Mastering Angular 19.2

Build Modern, Scalable Single-Page Applications Using TypeScript, HTML, and the Latest Angular Features

Kevin Stolz

Copyright Page

Table of Contents

Preface

When I first encountered Angular, I was captivated not just by its power, but by its philosophy. Here was a framework that didn't just offer a set of tools— it offered a structured way to build ambitious applications with clarity, modularity, and performance in mind. Over the years, Angular has grown, evolved, and matured—integrating new ideas, refining its architecture, and embracing innovations like standalone components and Signals. With Angular 19.2, the framework reaches an even higher level of developer productivity and scalability, making this the perfect time to master it.

This book, *Mastering Angular 19.2*, is written for developers who are serious about building real-world, production-grade applications using modern web standards. Whether you're transitioning from earlier Angular versions, migrating from another frontend framework, or just getting started with TypeScript-powered SPA development, this book is designed to guide you with both depth and clarity.

My goal in writing this book is not just to teach Angular as a collection of features or APIs, but to help you think in Angular. You'll not only understand *what* to do, but *why* it works that way—and how Angular's architecture can help you build scalable, maintainable, and testable single-page applications. The content is practical, code-heavy, and rooted in real-world scenarios that mirror what developers face every day. This is not a book of checklists or shallow tutorials—it's a full exploration of the framework in action.

You'll start by setting up a solid foundation: TypeScript, the Angular CLI, and best practices for working with components, forms, routing, and services. From there, we'll dive into advanced state management, modular architecture, performance optimization, testing strategies, and production deployment. Every concept is backed by hands-on examples and focused explanations, so you always know how to apply what you've learned.

Angular 19.2 introduces exciting improvements that simplify development and improve performance—from zoneless change detection to Signal-based reactivity. Throughout this book, we'll embrace those new tools and build modern applications that fully take advantage of what Angular offers today.

This book is for you if:

You want to build fast, scalable single-page applications using Angular.

You appreciate clear, well-structured guidance grounded in real development needs.

You're ready to move beyond surface-level knowledge and truly master the framework.

Thank you for picking up this book. I hope it becomes a reliable reference, a practical guide, and a trusted companion on your path to mastering Angular 19.2.

Let's build something amazing.

Chapter 1: Understanding Angular 19.2 in Context

Before we start writing any code, let's take a step back and understand what Angular really is, how it has evolved, and what makes **version 19.2** a particularly exciting release to master. Whether you're coming from React, Vue, or jQuery—or even an earlier version of Angular—you'll benefit from grounding yourself in what Angular stands for and how this version fits into its larger story.

A Brief History of Angular

Angular is a widely used web application framework developed and maintained by Google. Its history is unique because it involves two fundamentally different frameworks that share the same name. Understanding this distinction helps clarify the architecture and design decisions that shape modern Angular development today.

The first version, known as **AngularJS**, was released in 2010. It was created as a JavaScript-based framework for building dynamic, client-side web applications. AngularJS introduced powerful ideas at the time, such as **two-way data binding**, which automatically synchronized data between the model and the view; **dependency injection**, which allowed components to request their dependencies rather than create them; and **directives**, which let developers extend HTML with custom behavior. These features helped developers move away from manually updating the DOM and maintaining spaghetti code, especially in projects that required frequent data updates and UI reactivity.

However, AngularJS had several architectural limitations. As applications grew in complexity, developers began to experience performance issues, difficulty managing large codebases, and challenges in testing and maintainability. The framework relied heavily on dynamic scope-based models, and its change detection system, which used dirty checking, became increasingly inefficient with scale. It was clear that patching the existing codebase would not be sustainable in the long term.

Rather than incrementally updating AngularJS, the Angular team at Google decided to rebuild the framework from the ground up. In 2016, **Angular 2** was released. This was not an update but a completely new framework that abandoned AngularJS's architecture in favor of a modern, component-based approach using **TypeScript**—a statically typed superset of JavaScript developed by Microsoft. TypeScript brought the benefits of early error detection, better tooling, and clearer APIs. The new Angular was designed to be **modular**, **scalable**, and optimized for **performance**, making it suitable for enterprise-level applications.

To avoid confusion, AngularJS (the original) is often referred to as Angular 1.x, while the new, rewritten versions are simply called Angular, followed by their version number (e.g., Angular 2, Angular 4, Angular 12, and so on). There was no Angular 3—this version number was skipped to synchronize the versioning of the core libraries.

Since the release of Angular 2, the Angular team has followed a **regular release schedule**, delivering two major versions per year. Each version typically includes performance improvements, ergonomic enhancements, and new features, all introduced with a focus on backwards compatibility. This commitment has allowed organizations to confidently adopt Angular without worrying about frequent breaking changes.

Over time, the framework has introduced major improvements such as **Ivy**, the new rendering and compilation engine introduced in Angular 9, which reduced bundle sizes and improved debugging; **Standalone Components**, which simplify module dependencies; **typed reactive forms**, which strengthen type safety in form logic; and **Signals**, a more explicit and efficient reactivity model introduced in Angular 16 and further matured in Angular 19.

Angular today is one of the most fully-featured frameworks available. It provides a complete toolset for client-side development out of the box, including routing, HTTP handling, forms, dependency injection, state management patterns, and build tooling. It emphasizes structure, scalability, and testability—qualities that have made it a favorite among enterprise teams, public sector projects, and large-scale applications.

The story of Angular is not just about technological evolution, but about embracing modern development patterns while preserving stability. Each release builds on the foundation laid by the previous versions, guided by a strong emphasis on productivity, performance, and long-term maintainability.

Angular 19.2 continues this evolution, bringing refined support for Signals, improved developer tools, better performance through zoneless change detection, and a cleaner API surface. In this book, you will see how these advancements help you build modern, scalable single-page applications with clarity and confidence.

What's New in Angular 19.2

Angular 19.2 marks a significant point in the evolution of the Angular framework—not because it introduces an entirely new way of thinking, but because it refines and stabilizes some of the most important architectural changes Angular has seen in years. In this version, the core team has taken great care to mature features that were previously experimental, polish developer ergonomics, and push the performance boundaries even further— especially in large, component-heavy applications.

If you've been following recent Angular versions, you'll know that Signals have been one of the most transformative additions since the Ivy engine. Angular 19.2 brings Signals out of developer preview and into full, production-ready status. Signals give you a predictable, explicit, and performant way to manage reactive state in your applications. Unlike the older change detection mechanism that relies on zone-patching and broad reactivity through the component tree, Signals provide fine-grained reactivity—making it clearer when and why updates happen.

Let's look at what that means in practice.

Suppose you want to create a counter that doubles its value reactively whenever it changes. Previously, you might have reached for RxJS or local component state. With Signals, the same behavior becomes more predictable and easier to manage:

```
import { signal, computed } from '@angular/core';

export class CounterComponent {
  count = signal(0);
  doubled = computed(() => this.count() * 2);
```

```
  increment() {
    this.count.set(this.count() + 1);
  }
}
```

This setup ensures that whenever `count` changes, the `doubled` value is recomputed automatically. There's no subscription to manage, and no need to worry about unsubscribing when the component is destroyed. Angular knows how to track and clean up Signals automatically, which results in cleaner code and better performance.

Another key update in Angular 19.2 is its support for zoneless change detection. Angular has historically relied on Zone.js to monkey-patch browser APIs like `setTimeout` and `addEventListener` to know when to trigger change detection. While this has worked reliably for years, it often leads to performance overhead and opaque update cycles, especially in applications with high interactivity or custom rendering environments.

With 19.2, you now have native support for zoneless change detection. If you configure your app to work without Zone.js, Angular won't assume automatic updates after every asynchronous event. Instead, you can explicitly control when change detection runs, giving you the freedom to optimize performance in ways that were previously difficult.

Consider this scenario: you're building a dashboard that updates only when new data arrives over WebSocket. With zoneless mode, you can turn off automatic change detection and manually signal updates only when necessary:

```
import { ChangeDetectorRef } from '@angular/core';

constructor(private cdr: ChangeDetectorRef) {}

onNewDataReceived(data: any) {
  this.processData(data);
  this.cdr.detectChanges();
}
```

This level of control is powerful. It prevents unnecessary re-renders across your component tree and aligns Angular's behavior more closely with performance-sensitive environments like gaming dashboards, financial visualizations, or complex animation systems.

Routing improvements in Angular 19.2 are equally practical. You can now take advantage of fine-grained control over route lifecycle events. Developers often need to refresh data or reinitialize parts of the UI when route parameters change. In earlier versions of Angular, handling this required verbose code and workarounds using query parameter observers. Angular 19.2 introduces streamlined router hooks that allow you to intercept and manage route activations more directly, making things more predictable and readable.

For example, reloading data when the `id` parameter in a route changes is now much more straightforward. You can tie directly into the route lifecycle without wiring up complex subscriptions:

```
import { ActivatedRoute } from '@angular/router';

constructor(private route: ActivatedRoute) {
  this.route.params.subscribe(params => {
    const id = params['id'];
    this.loadData(id);
  });
}
```

While this code was possible before, the router now supports better activation management, especially when it comes to guards, data resolvers, and nested navigation patterns. These enhancements make Angular routing more aligned with real-world navigation needs, particularly in enterprise applications where control and predictability are essential.

There's also been substantial work done to streamline the development workflow itself. Angular CLI in 19.2 is more efficient, with better integration of **esbuild** for faster bundling and **Vite** as a modern dev server alternative. These changes speed up both development and production builds and open the door for more fine-grained control over the toolchain without sacrificing the CLI's ease of use.

Let's say you're building a component-heavy application with dozens of routes and hundreds of dependencies. In earlier Angular versions, build times could become sluggish, and incremental changes might take a few seconds to reflect. With the updated CLI, hot module reloading is snappier, cold builds are faster, and you'll find that working on large projects feels significantly more responsive.

Lastly, Angular 19.2 improves diagnostics and template type checking. Previously, developers could encounter silent errors in their templates—things like using undefined properties, incorrect binding names, or missing inputs—only at runtime or during complex debugging sessions. With the improvements introduced in this version, Angular catches these issues at compile time, giving you clearer feedback and reducing the likelihood of shipping broken UIs.

For example, if you mistakenly bind to a non-existent input on a component:

```
<app-user [nonexistentInput]="value"></app-user>
```

Angular 19.2 will now report this issue more explicitly during the build process, helping you resolve it early without hunting through the DOM at runtime.

In real-world teams, where multiple developers are working on shared components, this level of accuracy is invaluable. It reduces regressions, speeds up onboarding for new team members, and strengthens code integrity across large-scale applications.

Angular 19.2, in every way, is a developer-focused release. It brings polish, predictability, and performance enhancements without changing the core philosophy of the framework. If you're building enterprise-scale applications or care deeply about maintainability, type safety, and reactivity, this release provides the tools you need to work with confidence and precision.

In the chapters ahead, we'll use these new capabilities—Signals, zoneless change detection, improved routing, and CLI upgrades—to build a modern single-page application from the ground up. You'll get the opportunity to write, test, and deploy real code that benefits directly from the advancements introduced in Angular 19.2.

This is Angular at its most refined. And you're now fully equipped to start building with it.

Setting Up Your Development Environment

Before you start building with Angular 19.2, it's important to configure your development environment correctly. This setup process ensures that you'll have the right versions of each tool, access to debugging support, and smooth compatibility with Angular's ecosystem. A well-configured environment reduces friction and makes it easier to focus on writing your application logic rather than troubleshooting build errors or compatibility issues.

To work productively with Angular, you need four essential parts: Node.js and npm for managing packages and running the Angular CLI, the Angular CLI itself, a code editor with Angular support, and optionally, a browser extension or devtools for inspecting your running application. I'll guide you through each part, step by step.

Start by verifying that you have the correct version of Node.js installed. Angular 19.2 officially supports Node.js 18 LTS or newer. Type the following command in your terminal or command prompt:

```
node -v
```

If the result shows a version older than 18.x, or if Node is not recognized as a command, then you need to install it. You can download the recommended LTS version of Node.js from https://nodejs.org. Installing Node also gives you npm—the Node package manager—which is used to install and manage dependencies for Angular projects. Once installed, confirm that npm is available:

```
npm -v
```

Next, install the Angular CLI globally. The Angular CLI (Command Line Interface) is a powerful tool that simplifies everything from project scaffolding to building and deploying your application. It abstracts away complex configuration and provides a consistent structure for Angular apps. Use the following command to install it:

```
npm install -g @angular/cli
```

This installs the latest stable version of the CLI globally on your machine. You can check the installed version to ensure it aligns with Angular 19.2:

```
ng version
```

The output should list Angular CLI 19.2.x, along with other related packages like Angular core, RxJS, and TypeScript. If you've previously installed an older version of the CLI, upgrading is as simple as running:

```
npm install -g @angular/cli@19.2
```

Now that your CLI is set up, the next step is choosing a code editor. The most widely used and highly recommended editor for Angular development is **Visual Studio Code**. It's lightweight, free, and has an excellent ecosystem of extensions specifically tailored for Angular and TypeScript development.

You can download VS Code from https://code.visualstudio.com. Once installed, open the Extensions view and install the following:

Angular Language Service – provides intelligent autocompletion and real-time feedback for Angular templates.

ESLint – enables linting and code analysis to catch errors and enforce coding standards.

Prettier – handles automatic code formatting for a consistent code style.

Path Intellisense – enhances autocomplete when importing modules, assets, or components.

With these tools in place, you'll get rich intellisense inside HTML templates, real-time error checking, and consistent formatting—all of which significantly enhance your productivity and code quality.

Angular also benefits from having dedicated browser tools during development. Install **Angular DevTools**, which is available as a browser extension for Chrome and Edge. It lets you inspect component trees, see real-time signal and change detection data, and debug performance bottlenecks directly within your application. You can find the extension on the Chrome Web Store by searching for *Angular DevTools*.

To test that everything is configured correctly, create a new Angular project using the CLI. In your terminal, run:

```
ng new angular-19-app --standalone
```

The `--standalone` flag enables Angular's standalone components feature, introduced in earlier versions and now fully supported in 19.2. It simplifies the app structure by removing the need to create NgModules for every component. When prompted:

Choose **Yes** to enable Angular routing.

Select **SCSS** or **CSS** depending on your styling preference.

You can also choose **strict mode**, which is recommended for production-quality code.

Once the CLI finishes scaffolding your project, move into the project directory:

cd angular-19-app

Then start the development server:

ng serve

This will compile the application and launch it on `http://localhost:4200`. Open the browser and verify that you can see Angular's welcome page. From this point on, you can edit the app's components, see your changes reflected instantly, and start building real features.

To summarize, what you've set up is more than just a basic toolchain. You've laid the foundation for a modern development environment that aligns with Angular's best practices. Your setup includes proper versioning, an efficient CLI workflow, strong TypeScript support, intelligent code analysis, template debugging, and performance profiling—all configured and ready to go.

This environment will support you throughout this book, ensuring that the code you write compiles cleanly, runs efficiently, and follows Angular's evolving standards. In the next section, you'll begin working directly with Angular components, learning how to create, compose, and structure them for clarity and reuse. But for now, your tools are ready, your system is configured, and you're prepared to start building confidently with Angular 19.2.

Creating Your First Angular 19.2 Project

Now that your development environment is fully set up, you're ready to create your first Angular 19.2 project. This is a critical step—not just to validate your tooling, but to understand how Angular structures an application from the beginning. As we walk through this process together, you'll see how Angular's CLI scaffolds a clean, maintainable architecture, enabling you to focus on building functionality without wasting time on boilerplate configuration.

Let's begin by generating a new Angular project using the CLI. Open your terminal or command prompt and enter the following command:

```
ng new angular-19-app --standalone
```

Here, `angular-19-app` is the name of the project directory Angular will create for you, and the `--standalone` flag tells the CLI to use Angular's newer standalone component system instead of the traditional NgModule-based setup. Standalone components simplify Angular architecture by reducing the need for repetitive module definitions. They also promote a more component-driven mindset, which is central to modern Angular development.

Once you run the command, Angular CLI will prompt you with several options. The first asks whether you'd like to enable Angular routing. You should say **Yes**, because routing is a core feature of any single-page application, and you'll need it to navigate between different views in your app.

Next, the CLI will ask you to choose a stylesheet format. You can select from CSS, SCSS, SASS, LESS, or Stylus. If you're not sure, CSS is perfectly fine to begin with, but many developers prefer SCSS for its nesting and variable support. Once your choices are confirmed, Angular CLI begins scaffolding your project.

This process creates a fully functional Angular workspace. Open the new folder in Visual Studio Code:

```
cd angular-19-app
```

```
code .
```

At this point, the generated project includes several key files and directories:

src/main.ts: This is the entry point of your Angular application. It bootstraps the root component and starts rendering the app.

src/app/app.config.ts: This replaces the traditional `AppModule` in standalone apps. It declares providers and routing configuration.

src/app/app.component.ts: This is the root component. It controls the initial UI of your application.

angular.json: This is the CLI configuration file. It defines build settings, linting rules, and testing options.

package.json: This lists your project dependencies and scripts.

To confirm everything is working correctly, start the development server:

ng serve

The CLI will compile the app and launch a local development server on `http://localhost:4200`. Open that URL in your browser and you should see Angular's default welcome screen. This confirms that your project is correctly installed, the CLI is functioning, and Angular 19.2 is running as expected.

Now, let's begin customizing your application by editing the root component. In `src/app/app.component.ts`, you'll see a basic component setup:

```
import { Component } from '@angular/core';

@Component({
  selector: 'app-root',
  templateUrl: './app.component.html',
  styleUrl: './app.component.css',
  standalone: true
})
export class AppComponent {
  title = 'angular-19-app';
}
```

This class is decorated with `@Component`, which defines it as an Angular component. The `selector` tells Angular what tag to look for in the HTML to render this component. The `templateUrl` points to the HTML file where the component's template lives, and `standalone: true` marks it as a standalone component—meaning it doesn't need to be declared in any NgModule.

Open `app.component.html` and replace its contents with a simple welcome message and a button that increments a counter:

```
<h1>Welcome to Angular 19.2!</h1>

<p>You've just created your first Angular
application.</p>

<button (click)="increment()">Clicked {{ count }}
times</button>
```

Now open the `app.component.ts` file again and update the class to define the `count` and `increment` method using Angular Signals:

```
import { Component, signal } from '@angular/core';

@Component({
  selector: 'app-root',
  templateUrl: './app.component.html',
  styleUrl: './app.component.css',
  standalone: true
})
export class AppComponent {
  count = signal(0);

  increment() {
    this.count.set(this.count() + 1);
  }
}
```

This is your first practical use of **Signals** in Angular 19.2. Signals provide a reactive value that automatically triggers UI updates when the value changes. This example demonstrates how simple it is to bind application state to the view without needing RxJS or manual change detection triggers.

When you save these changes, your browser will refresh automatically. Click the button, and you'll see the counter increase. This confirms that event handling, reactivity, and template binding are all working correctly.

At this point, you've successfully:

Created an Angular 19.2 application with standalone components

Verified that routing and build systems are functioning

Written your first reactive component using Signals

Set the foundation for building scalable features with modern Angular architecture

This basic structure will carry forward into every part of your app. Components will manage UI and logic, templates will bind data and events, and Signals will help you maintain reactive state with minimal boilerplate.

Chapter 2: TypeScript and Modern Web Fundamentals

To truly master Angular 19.2, you need to be comfortable with more than just the Angular APIs—you need a solid grasp of **TypeScript** and the essential building blocks of the modern web: **HTML5** and **CSS3**. Angular is built with TypeScript at its core, and its most powerful features—like decorators, types, and tooling—are all enabled by TypeScript's capabilities. In this chapter, you and I will explore these foundations side-by-side, so that when you start architecting real features, the syntax and structure feel intuitive rather than mysterious.

Essential TypeScript for Angular

TypeScript is the foundation of Angular. Every component, service, directive, and module you create is written using TypeScript. It's not an optional layer added for safety—it's the language Angular was designed to work with. This means understanding TypeScript is not a nice-to-have skill; it's a requirement if you want to write clean, maintainable Angular applications.

Let's begin by getting clear on what TypeScript actually is. TypeScript is a statically typed superset of JavaScript. This means you still write JavaScript syntax, but with added features that allow you to define types for variables, function parameters, return values, and object structures. These types exist during development and compilation—they don't affect the final JavaScript that runs in the browser. Instead, they help catch errors early, improve code readability, and make your application easier to refactor and maintain.

When you're working on a real-world Angular app, you'll often need to describe the shape of data coming from an API, define component inputs and outputs, and implement services that communicate with other parts of your application. Doing all of this confidently requires you to use TypeScript features like type annotations, interfaces, enums, classes, and generics effectively. Let's work through each of these in a practical, Angular-oriented context.

Start with basic **type annotations**. When you define a variable, you can specify what kind of value it should hold. This prevents errors caused by passing the wrong type of data and allows your editor to provide better autocomplete and suggestions.

```
let username: string = 'Sarah';

let age: number = 28;

let isSubscribed: boolean = true;
```

If you try to assign a value of a different type to any of these variables, TypeScript will show a compile-time error:

```
age = 'twenty-eight'; // ✗ Error: Type 'string' is not assignable to type 'number'
```

In Angular, this kind of type safety becomes essential when handling form data or service responses. For example, if you're building a user profile form, you can create a typed object to hold the form's state:

```
type UserProfile = {
  name: string;
  email: string;
  age: number;
  isActive: boolean;
};

const user: UserProfile = {
  name: 'Jonah',
  email: 'jonah@example.com',
  age: 35,
  isActive: true
};
```

This structure lets you safely bind user properties to a template, confident that the correct types are being used throughout.

Next, consider functions. TypeScript allows you to specify both parameter and return types. This not only prevents misuse but also improves documentation directly in the function signature.

```
function greetUser(name: string): string {
  return `Hello, ${name}!`;
}
```

Angular frequently involves writing functions that process user input, handle HTTP responses, or transform data. With TypeScript, these functions can be typed to handle each case appropriately.

Let's now talk about **interfaces**. Interfaces let you describe the shape of an object more formally, and they're incredibly useful for service contracts or component inputs.

```
interface Product {

  id: number;

  name: string;

  price: number;

  available: boolean;

}
```

You might use this `Product` interface in a service that fetches product data from an API:

```
import { HttpClient } from '@angular/common/http';
import { Observable } from 'rxjs';

export class ProductService {
  constructor(private http: HttpClient) {}

  getAll(): Observable<Product[]> {
    return
this.http.get<Product[]>('/api/products');
  }
}
```

In this example, the interface not only defines what a `Product` looks like—it also ensures that every part of your code that deals with products knows exactly what properties are available, what types they are, and how to access them safely.

This approach avoids runtime surprises. If the server changes the shape of the response, your code will break during development—not in production.

Classes are the backbone of Angular components and services. TypeScript enhances JavaScript classes by supporting access modifiers like `public`, `private`, and `readonly`. This helps you enforce boundaries in your code and control how data flows between components.

Here's a simple component class:

```
export class CounterComponent {
  private _count = 0;

  get count(): number {
    return this._count;
  }

  increment(): void {
    this._count += 1;
  }
}
```

By marking `_count` as `private`, you're saying that this value should not be accessed or changed from outside the component. This level of encapsulation improves reliability by protecting internal state from accidental modifications.

Angular also relies heavily on **decorators**—functions prefixed with @ that attach metadata to classes. You've already seen `@Component` in the previous chapter. These decorators are part of Angular's design and use TypeScript's metadata reflection to enable features like dependency injection and template rendering.

```
import { Component } from '@angular/core';

@Component({
  selector: 'app-counter',
  template: `<button (click)="increment()">Clicked
{{ count }} times</button>`,
  standalone: true
})
export class CounterComponent {
  count = 0;

  increment() {
    this.count += 1;
```

```
    }
}
```

The `@Component` decorator tells Angular how to render and track this class. This is made possible by TypeScript's decorator support.

Let's now look at **enums**. Enums allow you to define a set of named constants. They're especially useful for dropdown values, states, or role types.

```
enum UserRole {

    Admin,

    Editor,

    Viewer

}


const role: UserRole = UserRole.Admin;
```

Enums help make code more readable and reduce errors from using arbitrary string values. If you're controlling access to routes or features in Angular, enums can help clarify which roles are permitted.

Finally, TypeScript's **generics** allow you to write functions and classes that work with a variety of types while preserving strict typing. Angular uses generics extensively—particularly in its HTTP module and RxJS observables.

Let's take an example that wraps an HTTP call:

```
getById<T>(url: string): Observable<T> {

    return this.http.get<T>(url);

}
```

This method allows you to specify the type of the expected result when calling it:

```
this.api.getById<Product>('/api/products/42').subsc
ribe(product => {
  console.log(product.name); // type-safe access to
`name`
});
```

Generics let you reuse logic while maintaining full type awareness. This is critical in Angular applications that rely on a variety of API calls and object types.

By writing Angular applications with TypeScript as your foundation, you gain more than just safety—you gain confidence. Your code becomes easier to understand, easier to test, and easier to refactor. And as your application grows, your use of types will protect you from common bugs and logic errors that can be difficult to catch through testing alone.

Using Interfaces, Generics, and Decorators

In Angular, your ability to write clean, scalable, and maintainable code depends heavily on how well you understand TypeScript's advanced features. Among these, **interfaces**, **generics**, and **decorators** stand out—not because they're abstract concepts, but because they are the backbone of how Angular structures its applications. Angular doesn't just use these features occasionally; it's designed around them.

Let's begin with **interfaces** because they define structure. Interfaces are how you describe the shape of an object in TypeScript. When working with real-world data—especially HTTP responses—you need a reliable way to define what that data should look like. Interfaces give you a contract that your code must follow, making your application more robust and your development experience more consistent.

Suppose your Angular app fetches a list of products from a backend API. Instead of relying on loose objects or any-type variables, you can define the structure of a Product using an interface:

```
interface Product {

  id: number;

  name: string;
```

```
  price: number;

  inStock: boolean;

}
```

This tells TypeScript: any object referred to as a `Product` must have those four properties, with those exact types. When this structure is applied in a service, it becomes much easier to reason about what the component should expect.

Here's a quick real-world use in a service:

```
import { Injectable } from '@angular/core';
import { HttpClient } from '@angular/common/http';
import { Observable } from 'rxjs';

@Injectable({ providedIn: 'root' })
export class ProductService {
  constructor(private http: HttpClient) {}

  getProducts(): Observable<Product[]> {
    return
this.http.get<Product[]>('/api/products');
  }
}
```

Now when a component subscribes to `getProducts()`, it knows that each object in the response will conform to the `Product` structure. If something doesn't match—if a field is missing or a type is wrong—TypeScript will catch it during development.

You're not just preventing bugs. You're documenting your application's data flows, enforcing consistency, and unlocking better code completion in your editor.

Now let's move on to **generics**. Generics allow you to write reusable code that works with different types while preserving type safety. In Angular, this is critical for services, utility classes, and even component logic.

For example, let's say you're building a service to manage local storage. You want to store and retrieve values of any type, but you still want the returned value to be strongly typed. That's where generics shine.

Here's a basic implementation:

```
export class LocalStorageService {
  setItem<T>(key: string, value: T): void {
    localStorage.setItem(key,
JSON.stringify(value));
  }

  getItem<T>(key: string): T | null {
    const item = localStorage.getItem(key);
    return item ? (JSON.parse(item) as T) : null;
  }
}
```

Now you can use the service with any type, and TypeScript will track what you're working with:

```
const user = { name: 'Amina', email:
'amina@example.com' };



storageService.setItem<User>('currentUser', user);



const storedUser =
storageService.getItem<User>('currentUser');

console.log(storedUser?.email); // Safe access with
full autocompletion
```

This pattern makes your code reusable without sacrificing strict typing. In a real-world Angular project, where multiple services deal with various data models, generics allow you to abstract logic without compromising safety or clarity.

Now let's talk about **decorators**. If you've written a component or a service in Angular, you've already used decorators like `@Component`, `@Injectable`, or `@Input`. But what are decorators, exactly?

In TypeScript, a decorator is a special kind of function that attaches metadata to classes, methods, or properties. Angular uses this metadata to understand how to process, instantiate, and wire up your classes at runtime.

Let's break down a basic `@Component` decorator:

```typescript
import { Component } from '@angular/core';

@Component({
  selector: 'app-profile-card',
  templateUrl: './profile-card.component.html',
  styleUrls: ['./profile-card.component.scss'],
  standalone: true
})
export class ProfileCardComponent {
  name = 'Ada Lovelace';
}
```

The `@Component` decorator provides Angular with the information it needs to treat `ProfileCardComponent` as a UI element. The `selector` defines the HTML tag you'll use to embed the component. The `templateUrl` points to the component's HTML structure. The `standalone` flag tells Angular that this component doesn't belong to a module and can be used independently.

What's important here is that decorators make Angular declarative. You don't register components manually or wire up dependencies imperatively. You annotate your classes, and Angular handles the rest. This leads to code that's not only easier to maintain but also easier to reason about, since the intent is clear and concise.

Another powerful decorator is `@Injectable`, which marks a class as available to Angular's dependency injection system:

```typescript
import { Injectable } from '@angular/core';

@Injectable({ providedIn: 'root' })
export class AuthService {
  login(email: string, password: string) {
    // authentication logic
  }
}
```

The `providedIn: 'root'` option tells Angular to make a single instance of this service available application-wide. This avoids the need to register the service in a module manually and enables tree-shaking for unused services.

Angular also supports method-level decorators like `@Input()` and `@Output()`, which are used for component communication. These allow data to flow between parent and child components, creating loosely coupled, modular UI structures.

```
import { Component, Input } from '@angular/core';

@Component({
  selector: 'app-user-greeting',
  template: `<p>Hello, {{ userName }}!</p>`,
  standalone: true
})
export class UserGreetingComponent {
  @Input() userName!: string;
}
```

Here, `@Input()` declares that the `userName` property can be passed into the component from its parent. Angular wires this up at runtime based on the metadata provided by the decorator.

These decorators are more than just syntax—they're what makes Angular work. They enable dependency injection, dynamic component loading, template parsing, and more. When you use them correctly, your code becomes clearer and more aligned with Angular's architectural principles.

By combining interfaces, generics, and decorators, you unlock the full potential of Angular's development model. Interfaces let you define structure and catch mistakes early. Generics give you reusable logic with precise types. Decorators enable declarative architecture that's easy to understand and extend.

You'll use these tools constantly as you build components, communicate between them, fetch data, and manage state. Mastering them doesn't just make you more proficient with Angular—it makes your applications more stable, scalable, and maintainable.

Strict Typing and Compilation

Strict typing is one of the most powerful features TypeScript brings to Angular—and it becomes even more valuable as your application grows. With strict typing enabled, you reduce the chance of silent errors, enforce discipline in your code, and gain the full advantage of TypeScript's static analysis during development. Angular 19.2 supports strict typing across its templates, components, services, and forms, and it integrates this deeply into the compiler.

Let's explore what strict typing actually means, how Angular uses it, and why enabling it at the start of your project will save you hours of debugging and refactoring later.

When you create a new Angular project using the CLI, you're asked if you want to enable strict mode. If you say yes, Angular configures your tsconfig.json file and additional settings to activate strict typing throughout your project. If you skipped that step or are upgrading from an older project, you can still enable strict mode manually.

In your tsconfig.json, you'll find this block:

```
{

  "compilerOptions": {

    "strict": true,

    "strictNullChecks": true,

    "noImplicitAny": true,

    "alwaysStrict": true,

    "strictFunctionTypes": true,

    "strictBindCallApply": true,

    "strictPropertyInitialization": true

  }
```

```
}
```

Each of these flags enforces a specific rule about how values are declared, assigned, and used. For instance, `noImplicitAny` ensures that TypeScript doesn't silently infer the `any` type when it can't determine a variable's type. Instead, it forces you to be explicit, which makes your code safer and easier to refactor.

Let's say you define a function without specifying parameter types:

```
function greet(user) {

  return `Hello, ${user.name}`;

}
```

In non-strict mode, this compiles—but `user` has the `any` type, which disables type checking for that variable. You could accidentally call `user.abc()` even if it doesn't exist, and TypeScript won't warn you. In strict mode, this code fails to compile until you provide a clear type:

```
interface User {
  name: string;
}

function greet(user: User): string {
  return `Hello, ${user.name}`;
}
```

Now TypeScript enforces that `user` must have a `name` property of type `string`. Any call to `greet()` must pass in a properly structured object. This guarantees consistency, and it gives your editor full awareness of what you're working with.

Strict typing becomes even more critical when handling **null** and **undefined** values. Without strict mode, TypeScript may let you pass `null` where a value is required, leading to unexpected runtime failures. With `strictNullChecks`, the compiler makes you explicitly handle these cases.

For example:

```
function getLength(text: string | null): number {
```

```
    return text.length; // ✗ Object is possibly
'null'
}
```

This won't compile in strict mode. You must first confirm that text is not null:

```
function getLength(text: string | null): number {
    return text ? text.length : 0;
}
```

This is especially useful in Angular templates, where you often bind to variables that may be loaded asynchronously. Suppose you have a component that fetches a user profile and displays the name in the template:

```
<p>{{ user.name }}</p>
```

If user is initially undefined while waiting for an API call to complete, the above line would throw an error at runtime. With strict template type checking enabled, Angular warns you about this during compilation:

Property 'name' does not exist on type 'undefined'.

To fix it safely, you might update your template like this:

```
<p *ngIf="user">{{ user.name }}</p>
```

Or better yet, use the **optional chaining operator**:

```
<p>{{ user?.name }}</p>
```

This small change ensures that Angular doesn't try to access the name property if user is still undefined. You don't have to wait for runtime surprises— Angular tells you at build time that the variable might be null or undefined, and it helps you address it early.

Strict typing also improves Angular's **template type checking**. By default, Angular performs basic type checking in templates, but with strict mode, it goes deeper. It understands component class members, verifies input and output bindings, checks directive usage, and validates structural directive syntax.

Consider this component:

```
@Component({
  selector: 'app-article',
  template: `<p>{{ article.title }}</p>`,
  standalone: true
})
export class ArticleComponent {
  article?: { title: string };
}
```

In strict mode, Angular immediately flags that `article` may be `undefined`, and it prevents the template from compiling until the issue is resolved. This protects you from subtle bugs like undefined property errors when rendering components.

Now let's take a practical example that reflects a common Angular use case. Suppose you are building a service that communicates with an external API. You receive a list of posts and display them in a blog feed.

Here's your model:

```
interface BlogPost {

  id: number;

  title: string;

  content: string;

  author?: string;

}
```

Your service might look like this:

```
@Injectable({ providedIn: 'root' })
export class BlogService {
  constructor(private http: HttpClient) {}

  getPosts(): Observable<BlogPost[]> {
    return this.http.get<BlogPost[]>('/api/posts');
  }
}
```

And your component:

```
@Component({
  selector: 'app-blog-feed',
  templateUrl: './blog-feed.component.html',
  standalone: true
})
export class BlogFeedComponent implements OnInit {
  posts: BlogPost[] = [];

  constructor(private blogService: BlogService) {}

  ngOnInit(): void {
    this.blogService.getPosts().subscribe(data => {
      this.posts = data;
    });
  }
}
```

In your template:

```
<ul>

  <li *ngFor="let post of posts">

    <h2>{{ post.title }}</h2>

    <p>{{ post.content }}</p>

    <small *ngIf="post.author">By {{ post.author
}}</small>

  </li>

</ul>
```

With strict typing enabled, Angular ensures that:

The service response structure matches the BlogPost interface.

The component accesses only the fields that exist on BlogPost.

The template doesn't access a possibly undefined property (author) without a check.

You get safety, clarity, and a better developer experience—all enforced at compile time.

To enable strict template checks explicitly, you can update angularCompilerOptions in tsconfig.json:

```
"angularCompilerOptions": {

  "strictTemplates": true

}
```

This activates Angular's most advanced template validation, catching issues like invalid property access, unrecognized bindings, and structural directive misuse.

Strict typing and compilation are not about writing more code—they're about writing **correct** code. You prevent entire categories of bugs before your application even runs. You gain confidence when refactoring. You document your code naturally through types. And in Angular, the benefits extend across your services, components, inputs, forms, and templates.

As you build out larger features, you'll appreciate having TypeScript and Angular's compiler as your first line of defense. You'll ship fewer bugs, catch edge cases early, and produce code that other developers can understand without asking questions.

HTML5 and CSS3 Essentials for Angular Apps

When you build Angular applications, you're not working in isolation from the browser. Angular provides structure and logic, but the actual interface—the part users interact with—is still built with **HTML5** and **CSS3**. These aren't secondary concerns. They're central to the experience you're delivering. And while Angular gives you a powerful component-based architecture, it does not replace the need to understand and use modern HTML and CSS effectively.

Let's start with **HTML5**. HTML is how you structure your application's content. Angular templates are HTML files enriched with Angular syntax—binding expressions, directives, and dynamic rendering—but the base is still

35

HTML. If your HTML structure is weak, confusing, or inaccessible, no amount of Angular logic will fix that. So it's important to use HTML elements semantically and intentionally.

Here's a basic Angular component template that uses standard HTML5 elements to display a user profile:

```
<section class="profile-card">
  <header>
    <h1>{{ user.name }}</h1>
    <p>{{ user.email }}</p>
  </header>

  <article>
    <h2>Bio</h2>
    <p>{{ user.bio }}</p>
  </article>

  <footer>
    <button (click)="logout()">Logout</button>
  </footer>
</section>
```

This template uses `<section>`, `<header>`, `<article>`, and `<footer>` to give structure to the content. These are semantic elements introduced in HTML5. They help not just with accessibility (for screen readers and keyboard navigation) but also with search engine optimization and long-term maintainability. Every tag communicates meaning, not just layout.

Angular enhances this HTML with bindings. `{{ user.name }}` is Angular's interpolation syntax—it inserts dynamic values from the component class into the DOM. But the structure, the tags, and the overall semantic design still come from HTML5.

Angular also supports all standard HTML5 form elements. This is important when working with template-driven or reactive forms. Input validation attributes like `required`, `minlength`, `pattern`, and `type` integrate naturally into Angular's validation system.

Take this form, for example:

```
<form (ngSubmit)="submit()" #userForm="ngForm">
```

```
  <input
    type="email"
    name="email"
    ngModel
    required
    placeholder="Enter your email"
  />
  <button type="submit"
[disabled]="userForm.invalid">Submit</button>
</form>
```

Here, HTML5 attributes (type="email" and required) combine with Angular directives (ngModel, ngSubmit, #userForm="ngForm") to build a reactive, validated form with minimal code. This blending of standards and framework features is a core strength of Angular—it never forces you to choose between the web platform and the framework.

Now let's shift to **CSS3**, which is what defines the visual styling of your components. Angular doesn't impose a particular styling method. You can use plain CSS, SCSS, or any preprocessor you prefer. The key thing Angular does offer is **style encapsulation**. Styles declared in a component's .css or .scss file apply only to that component by default.

Here's an example. Suppose you have a component called UserCardComponent with this template:

```
<div class="card">

  <h2>{{ name }}</h2>

  <p>{{ email }}</p>

</div>
```

And the accompanying stylesheet user-card.component.css:

```
.card {

  padding: 16px;

  background-color: #f7f7f7;
```

37

```
  border-radius: 8px;

  box-shadow: 0 2px 4px rgba(0, 0, 0, 0.1);

}
```

This `.card` class will not affect other components in your application. Angular automatically scopes these styles using attributes like `_ngcontent-abc`, which are added at runtime. This means you can name classes freely without worrying about global conflicts or cascading side effects.

If you want to use global styles—for layout frameworks, utility classes, or base typography—you can define them in `src/styles.scss` and include them in `angular.json`. But component styles should remain local for clarity and safety.

Angular supports all CSS3 layout and animation features. This includes **Flexbox**, **Grid**, **media queries**, and **CSS transitions**. If you want a responsive layout that adapts to screen sizes, you can write it using standard media queries inside component styles:

```
@media screen and (max-width: 768px) {

  .card {

    padding: 12px;

    font-size: 14px;

  }

}
```

For more structured layouts, CSS Grid works beautifully with Angular components:

```
.container {

  display: grid;

  grid-template-columns: 1fr 2fr;

  gap: 20px;
```

```
}
```

This approach lets you build clean, adaptable UIs without JavaScript layout hacks. You can also combine Angular's structural directives with CSS for dynamic visibility and layout control:

```
<div *ngIf="isLoading" class="spinner"></div>
.spinner {
  width: 40px;
  height: 40px;
  border: 4px solid #ccc;
  border-top-color: #1976d2;
  border-radius: 50%;
  animation: spin 0.8s linear infinite;
}

@keyframes spin {
  to {
    transform: rotate(360deg);
  }
}
```

This gives you smooth, CSS-powered animations that respond to Angular state changes without writing a single line of imperative animation logic.

In large applications, it's a good practice to use **CSS variables** for theming. These can be defined globally and referenced across components:

```
:root {

  --primary-color: #1976d2;

  --accent-color: #ff4081;

}
```

And used like this:

```
button {

  background-color: var(--primary-color);

  color: #fff;
```

```
}
```

You can even dynamically change these values at runtime—for example, in response to dark mode toggles—by modifying them with JavaScript or using Angular host bindings.

Angular also supports **view encapsulation modes**. By default, Angular uses **Emulated** encapsulation, which scopes styles using attributes. If you want to use global styles or integrate with legacy CSS, you can disable encapsulation on a component like this:

```
@Component({
    selector: 'app-header',
    templateUrl: './header.component.html',
    styleUrls: ['./header.component.css'],
    encapsulation: ViewEncapsulation.None,
    standalone: true
})
export class HeaderComponent {}
```

This causes the component's styles to behave like regular global CSS. Use this with caution—it's helpful when integrating with third-party libraries or global design systems, but for most use cases, scoped styles are safer.

To summarize the principle: **Angular gives you structure; HTML5 and CSS3 give you expression**. If you write meaningful markup and use modern CSS features in combination with Angular's powerful component architecture, you'll produce apps that are responsive, accessible, and visually consistent.

Everything you build in Angular will use these technologies. So whether you're styling a login form, building a data grid, or laying out a dashboard, a strong command of HTML5 and CSS3 will directly improve the quality of your application.

Chapter 3: Building with Components and Templates

In Angular, **components** are the fundamental building blocks of any application. Every visible element, interactive widget, or layout section you construct is made from components. They're not just organizational units—they define what users see and how they interact with the interface. When you understand how to write clear, efficient components, you gain the ability to build scalable and maintainable applications.

The Role of Components in Angular

In Angular, **components** are the foundation of everything you build. Every piece of your application's user interface—from a button to a navigation bar to an entire page—is created and controlled through components. Angular treats each component as a self-contained unit that defines its own structure, style, and behavior. Understanding components thoroughly isn't just helpful—it's essential if you want to write Angular applications that are scalable, maintainable, and predictable.

At a technical level, a component in Angular is a TypeScript class decorated with metadata that tells Angular how it should be used and rendered. This metadata includes the component's selector (the custom HTML tag name you'll use in templates), the path to its HTML template, and the location of its CSS styles.

Let's begin with a simple component example to ground this idea in code:

```
import { Component } from '@angular/core';

@Component({
  selector: 'app-greeting',
  template: `<h1>Hello, {{ name }}!</h1>`,
  styleUrls: ['./greeting.component.css'],
  standalone: true
})
export class GreetingComponent {
  name = 'Angular Developer';
}
```

This class defines a component named `GreetingComponent`. It has a single property, `name`, which is bound into the template using Angular's interpolation syntax (`{{ name }}`). The `@Component` decorator tells Angular that this class should be treated as a component, and provides the configuration needed to render it.

When you include `<app-greeting></app-greeting>` in another template, Angular renders this component's HTML into the DOM and binds the `name` property to the view automatically.

Every Angular application starts with a root component, usually called `AppComponent`. This root component sits at the top of the component tree. Every other component in your application is either a child or descendant of this root. By organizing your interface into a tree of components, you gain precise control over each unit of the UI.

This structure allows you to encapsulate responsibility. One component handles the navigation menu. Another handles a login form. A third might be responsible for a dashboard chart. These components each manage their own state, logic, and presentation, and Angular handles composing them together to build a complete interface.

Because Angular components are so modular, they promote **reusability**. When a piece of UI is needed in multiple places—for example, a user profile badge or a loading spinner—you can extract that piece into its own component and use it wherever needed by referencing its selector.

Suppose you're building an admin panel. You might create a component like this:

```
@Component({
  selector: 'app-user-summary',
  template: `
    <div class="user-summary">
      <h2>{{ user.name }}</h2>
      <p>{{ user.email }}</p>
    </div>
  `,
  standalone: true
})
export class UserSummaryComponent {
```

```
  @Input() user!: { name: string; email: string };
}
```

This component displays summary information for a user. The `@Input()` decorator marks `user` as a property that should be passed in from a parent component. This allows the `UserSummaryComponent` to be reused anywhere in your application and receive data dynamically.

In a parent component, you can include this component like so:

```
<app-user-summary [user]="selectedUser"></app-user-summary>
```

Angular components are also the foundation for **user interaction**. You can bind to DOM events such as clicks, form submissions, and keyboard input directly in the template using event bindings. For instance:

```
<button (click)="increment()">Add</button>

<p>Count: {{ count }}</p>
```

And in the corresponding class:

```
export class CounterComponent {
  count = 0;

  increment() {
    this.count++;
  }
}
```

The event handler method `increment()` updates the internal `count` state, which automatically re-renders in the view because Angular tracks these changes through its reactivity system.

Angular ensures that each component's style is scoped only to that component by default. This means styles you define in one component won't accidentally leak into others. This style encapsulation is handled behind the scenes through attributes like `_ngcontent-*`, but you don't need to manage that manually. It just works. You get modular styles, no conflicts, and the flexibility to build your app piece by piece without worrying about CSS collisions.

Angular also allows components to host **child components**. This nesting of components creates a hierarchy where the parent can pass data into the child, and the child can emit events back to the parent. This parent-child communication pattern is one of the most important skills to develop when building with Angular, because it enables your app to function as a collection of isolated, interactive pieces that communicate in a predictable and type-safe way.

As an example, suppose you have a `ProductListComponent` that shows a list of products and a `ProductItemComponent` that renders each individual product. The parent can pass product data to each child, and the child can notify the parent when the user clicks "Add to Cart".

The item component might look like this:

```
@Component({
   selector: 'app-product-item',
   template: `
     <div class="product">
        <h3>{{ product.name }}</h3>
        <p>{{ product.price | currency }}</p>
        <button (click)="addToCart()">Add to
Cart</button>
     </div>
   `,
   standalone: true
})
export class ProductItemComponent {
   @Input() product!: { name: string; price: number
};
   @Output() add = new EventEmitter<void>();

   addToCart() {
     this.add.emit();
   }
}
```

And in the parent component:

```
<app-product-item
   *ngFor="let item of products"
   [product]="item"
```

```
    (add)="onAddToCart(item)"
></app-product-item>
```

This level of modularity and event-driven design is made possible entirely through Angular components.

Components are not just visual units—they are the containers of logic, the endpoints of interaction, and the coordinators of application behavior. When you break your app into thoughtfully designed components, you make it easier to develop features independently, isolate bugs, and improve performance by updating only what's necessary.

Every Angular feature—routing, forms, HTTP communication, animations— is ultimately expressed through components. If you understand components well, you understand Angular.

Now that you've seen how central components are to Angular's architecture, we can move forward and explore how **standalone components** and **Signals** make these building blocks even more powerful in Angular 19.2. These features simplify your design and provide a more predictable development experience, especially when dealing with complex UI logic and application state.

Standalone Components and Signals in Angular 19.2

Angular 19.2 continues to simplify development by fully embracing **standalone components** and **Signals**—two features that not only reduce boilerplate, but also introduce more predictability and performance into how Angular applications are built and updated.

These features are not isolated improvements. They change how you think about architecting your app. They encourage smaller, more focused pieces of UI logic, with fewer dependencies and more explicit reactivity. And when combined, they significantly improve the clarity of both your code and your application's runtime behavior.

Standalone Components: No More Module Declarations

Prior to Angular 14, components had to be declared inside an NgModule. That meant every component, directive, or pipe had to be listed in the `declarations` array of a module, and modules had to import other modules to access shared functionality. It worked—but as projects grew, the module system became a source of friction. Dependencies could get tangled, tree-shaking became less effective, and reusability suffered when trying to pull components across module boundaries.

With Angular's new standalone API, you can define a component without attaching it to any NgModule. A standalone component declares its own dependencies. That means it knows which common directives or components it uses, and it imports only what it needs—no more relying on external modules to provide them.

Here's an example of a standalone component that displays a message:

```
import { Component } from '@angular/core';

@Component({
  selector: 'app-message',
  standalone: true,
  template: `<p>{{ message }}</p>`
})
export class MessageComponent {
  message = 'Hello from a standalone component!';
}
```

There's no module declaration. You can now import this component directly into any route, feature module, or parent component.

If this component needs other functionality—like `NgIf`, `NgFor`, `FormsModule`, or a shared library—it imports those explicitly via the `imports` array in the decorator:

```
import { CommonModule } from '@angular/common';

@Component({
  selector: 'app-notice',
  standalone: true,
  imports: [CommonModule],
  template: `
```

```
    <p *ngIf="visible">This is a conditionally
visible notice.</p>
`
})
export class NoticeComponent {
  visible = true;
}
```

This way, the component explicitly declares its template dependencies, making it easier to reason about and test in isolation. It also improves IDE support and enables better static analysis during build.

Standalone components are particularly effective for building reusable UI libraries. You can ship a component that's truly self-contained—just import it where needed without worrying about which module it belongs to.

Angular 19.2 promotes this architecture as a first-class pattern. When you create a new project using the CLI with `--standalone`, even your `AppComponent` will be standalone by default. Routing, bootstrapping, and lazy-loading also support standalone components seamlessly.

Here's how you might configure routing with standalone components:

```
export const routes: Routes = [
  { path: '', component: HomeComponent },
  { path: 'about', loadComponent: () =>
import('./about.component').then(m =>
m.AboutComponent) }
];
```

This is direct and clean—no module indirection, no lazy-loaded NgModule wrappers. Just component-driven routes.

Signals: Fine-Grained Reactivity, Simplified

While standalone components simplify structure, **Signals** address the way state changes are tracked and reflected in the UI.

Traditionally, Angular used zone-based change detection. Any asynchronous event—like a `setTimeout`, HTTP response, or user interaction—would trigger a full application change detection cycle. Angular would check every binding in every component to see what changed. While this worked, it could be inefficient, especially in performance-critical scenarios.

Signals change that.

A **Signal** is a reactive state holder. It behaves like a variable, but it tracks who reads from it. When you update a Signal, only the components or templates that depend on it are notified and re-evaluated.

Let's look at a counter component that uses Signals:

```
import { Component, signal } from '@angular/core';

@Component({
  selector: 'app-counter',
  standalone: true,
  template: `
    <p>Count: {{ count() }}</p>
    <button (click)="increment()">Add</button>
  `
})
export class CounterComponent {
  count = signal(0);

  increment() {
    this.count.set(this.count() + 1);
  }
}
```

count is a Signal initialized with the value 0. In the template, we read the value using count(). Whenever count.set() is called, Angular automatically re-renders only the parts of the view that depend on that Signal. There's no need to manually trigger change detection or rely on @Input updates or ngOnChanges.

Signals are synchronous, predictable, and don't require you to manage subscriptions. They provide an alternative to BehaviorSubject and RxJS in many use cases where full stream management isn't necessary.

You can also create **computed Signals**. These are derived values that automatically update when their dependencies change:

```
import { computed } from '@angular/core';

@Component({
  selector: 'app-double-counter',
  standalone: true,
  template: `<p>Double: {{ doubled() }}</p>`
})
export class DoubleCounterComponent {
  count = signal(2);
  doubled = computed(() => this.count() * 2);
}
```

If count changes, doubled updates automatically. No boilerplate, no observable pipelines.

And when you want side effects, you can use effect():

```
import { effect } from '@angular/core';

@Component({
  selector: 'app-logger',
  standalone: true,
  template: `<button
(click)="increment()">+</button>`
})
export class LoggerComponent {
  count = signal(0);

  constructor() {
    effect(() => {
      console.log('Count changed:', this.count());
    });
  }

  increment() {
    this.count.update(n => n + 1);
  }
}
```

This effect will run every time count changes. You can use it for logging, analytics, local storage, or triggering logic outside of rendering.

In Angular 19.2, Signals are fully stable and integrated into forms, templates, change detection, and developer tooling. They provide the missing piece for building Angular applications that are both fast and easy to understand.

Standalone components and Signals aren't just feature additions—they represent a shift in Angular's design philosophy toward **simplicity**, **predictability**, and **modularity**. By reducing the need for modules and zone-based updates, Angular gives you finer control over your app's structure and reactivity, without losing the benefits of its underlying framework.

You don't need to replace every existing pattern in your app with Signals and standalone components immediately. But as you write new features or refactor old ones, adopting these tools will help you write code that's easier to debug, test, and maintain.

Data Binding, Directives, and Structural Templates

In Angular, the connection between your logic and the browser interface is handled through **data binding** and **directives**. These are not superficial conveniences—they are the tools that allow you to build interfaces that update dynamically in response to changes in state, user actions, or external data sources. Templates in Angular are more than static HTML—they are dynamic, expressive views that integrate tightly with your component's properties and methods.

This section will give you a practical and detailed understanding of how data flows between your component class and its HTML, how Angular responds to user interaction, and how structural directives like `*ngIf` and `*ngFor` transform the DOM in intelligent ways.

Data Binding: Connecting Component State to the Template

Angular offers four main types of data binding: **interpolation**, **property binding**, **event binding**, and **two-way binding**. Each serves a specific purpose, and together they create a highly reactive UI system.

Interpolation allows you to embed expressions into the HTML using double curly braces (`{{ }}`). It's used to display dynamic text.

```
export class WelcomeComponent {

  name = 'Nehemiah';

}
```

```
<h1>Welcome, {{ name }}!</h1>
```

Angular evaluates the expression inside {{ name }} and updates the DOM whenever name changes. This is one-way binding from the component to the view.

Property binding uses square brackets ([ ]) to bind DOM properties to component values. This allows you to set things like src, disabled, value, and custom properties on components.

```
export class ProfileComponent {

  avatarUrl = '/assets/user.png';

}
```

```
<img [src]="avatarUrl" />
```

If avatarUrl changes in your component, Angular automatically updates the src attribute in the DOM.

Event binding uses parentheses (( )) to listen for DOM events and execute methods in your component.

```
export class ClickTrackerComponent {
  count = 0;

  increment() {
    this.count++;
  }
}
<button (click)="increment()">Clicked {{ count }}
times</button>
```

Here, when the user clicks the button, Angular calls the increment() method and updates the count in the view automatically. The binding is from the view to the component.

Two-way binding combines property and event binding using the `[( )]` syntax. This is primarily used in form controls with the `ngModel` directive.

```
export class FeedbackComponent {

  message = '';

}

<textarea [(ngModel)]="message"></textarea>

<p>You typed: {{ message }}</p>
```

This creates a bidirectional connection. When the user types into the textarea, `message` updates. When `message` changes in the component, the input field reflects that change. It's useful for building forms, live editors, or any input-bound interface.

Directives: Enhancing Behavior and Appearance

Angular directives are instructions you place on elements to modify their behavior or appearance. There are three types: **component directives**, **attribute directives**, and **structural directives**. In this section, we'll focus on attribute and structural directives since they directly affect templates.

Attribute directives modify the appearance or behavior of an element without changing the structure. A common example is `ngClass`:

```
export class TaskComponent {

  isCompleted = true;

}

<p [ngClass]="{ 'completed': isCompleted }">Task 1</p>
```

If `isCompleted` is true, Angular adds the class `completed` to the paragraph tag. You can define the style in your CSS:

```
.completed {
  text-decoration: line-through;
  color: gray;
```

```
}
```

Another example is `ngStyle`, which applies styles dynamically:

```
<p [ngStyle]="{ color: isCompleted ? 'gray' :
'black' }">Task 2</p>
```

Attribute directives give you granular control over styling and behavior in response to state without manipulating the DOM manually.

Structural Directives: Shaping the DOM

Structural directives affect layout by adding or removing elements from the DOM. These are the ones with an asterisk prefix, such as `*ngIf` and `*ngFor`.

The `*ngIf` directive conditionally includes or excludes a block based on a boolean expression.

```
export class AuthComponent {

   isLoggedIn = false;

}

<p *ngIf="isLoggedIn">Welcome back!</p>

<p *ngIf="!isLoggedIn">Please log in.</p>
```

Angular evaluates the expression and either includes the element or removes it entirely from the DOM.

You can also assign the result of the condition to a local variable:

```
<p *ngIf="user as currentUser">Hello, {{
currentUser.name }}</p>
```

This is useful when you're checking if a value exists and also want to reference it inside the same block.

The `*ngFor` directive creates a template for each item in a collection:

```
export class ProductListComponent {
  products = [
    { name: 'Laptop', price: 1200 },
```

```
    { name: 'Phone', price: 800 },
    { name: 'Tablet', price: 500 }
  ];
}
<ul>
  <li *ngFor="let product of products">
    {{ product.name }} - ${{ product.price }}
  </li>
</ul>
```

Angular repeats the `<li>` element for each object in the `products` array. You can also access additional context like index or whether the item is the first or last:

```
<li *ngFor="let product of products; let i = index;
let last = last">

  {{ i + 1 }}. {{ product.name }} <span
*ngIf="last">(last item)</span>

</li>
```

This makes it easy to build lists, tables, dropdowns, and menus—all driven by real-time data.

Combining Binding and Structure in Real Applications

Let's walk through a practical example. Suppose you're building a todo list. Here's how data binding and structural directives work together in a full-featured component.

Component class:

```
export class TodoComponent {
  todos = [
    { task: 'Write documentation', done: false },
    { task: 'Push code to GitHub', done: true }
  ];

  newTask = '';

  addTask() {
    if (this.newTask.trim()) {
```

54

```
      this.todos.push({ task: this.newTask, done:
false });
      this.newTask = '';
    }
  }

  toggleDone(index: number) {
    this.todos[index].done =
!this.todos[index].done;
  }
}
```

Template:

```
<h2>Todo List</h2>
<input [(ngModel)]="newTask" placeholder="New task"
/>
<button (click)="addTask()">Add</button>

<ul>
  <li *ngFor="let todo of todos; let i = index">
    <label>
      <input type="checkbox" [checked]="todo.done"
(change)="toggleDone(i)" />
      <span [ngClass]="{ done: todo.done }">{{
todo.task }}</span>
    </label>
  </li>
</ul>
```

CSS:

```
.done {

  text-decoration: line-through;

  color: gray;

}
```

This is a complete, interactive UI built entirely with Angular's data binding and directives. No third-party state management, no imperative DOM manipulation. Angular handles reactivity, event handling, DOM updates, and styling—all while maintaining a clear separation between logic and layout.

Mastering Angular's data binding and template syntax is what transforms your components from static placeholders into interactive tools. Templates are not just a place to write HTML. They are dynamic views powered by Angular's change detection, designed to stay in sync with your application state and respond to the user in real time.

Component Communication and Reusability

In Angular, components don't exist in isolation. As your application grows, your components will need to interact with one another—sharing data, triggering events, and coordinating behaviors. This is a critical part of building scalable, maintainable applications. When you design components to be reusable and composable, you're making your application easier to extend, debug, and test. But for that to work, you need a solid understanding of how components **communicate**.

Communication in Angular follows a clear, predictable pattern based on **inputs** and **outputs**. A parent component passes data into a child using `@Input()`, and the child can emit events back to the parent using `@Output()` and `EventEmitter`. This unidirectional flow is straightforward, predictable, and fully type-safe, making it ideal for building interfaces that are both dynamic and modular.

Passing Data with @Input()

Suppose you have a `UserCardComponent` that's responsible for displaying a user's basic profile information. You want it to be reusable, meaning the data it displays should be determined by whatever parent component is using it.

In the child component, you define an `@Input()` property:

```
import { Component, Input } from '@angular/core';

@Component({
  selector: 'app-user-card',
  standalone: true,
  template: `
    <div class="user-card">
```

```
      <h3>{{ user.name }}</h3>
      <p>{{ user.email }}</p>
    </div>
  `
})
export class UserCardComponent {
  @Input() user!: { name: string; email: string };
}
```

The @Input() decorator tells Angular that the user property will be set by the parent component. The exclamation mark (!) asserts that Angular will definitely assign this property before it's accessed.

Now in a parent component, you can use the UserCardComponent like this:

```
export class UserListComponent {

  selectedUser = { name: 'Jane Doe', email:
'jane@example.com' };

}

<app-user-card [user]="selectedUser"></app-user-
card>
```

The parent binds its selectedUser object to the child's user property using property binding syntax [user]="selectedUser". When selectedUser changes, Angular automatically updates the child's input. This is one-way binding—data flows from parent to child.

Sending Events with @Output()

Now let's say your UserCardComponent includes a delete button. When the user clicks it, you want to notify the parent so it can handle the deletion logic.

You do this using @Output() and EventEmitter.

Inside UserCardComponent:

```
import { Output, EventEmitter } from
'@angular/core';

@Component({
```

```
  selector: 'app-user-card',
  standalone: true,
  template: `
    <div class="user-card">
      <h3>{{ user.name }}</h3>
      <p>{{ user.email }}</p>
      <button
(click)="deleteUser()">Delete</button>
    </div>
  `
})
export class UserCardComponent {
  @Input() user!: { name: string; email: string };
  @Output() delete = new EventEmitter<void>();

  deleteUser() {
    this.delete.emit();
  }
}
```

In the parent template:

```
<app-user-card

  [user]="selectedUser"

  (delete)="removeUser(selectedUser)"

></app-user-card>
```

When the child emits the `delete` event, the parent receives it and calls `removeUser(selectedUser)`. This pattern gives you a clean separation of responsibilities: the child handles the UI and emits intent; the parent handles business logic and state changes.

Reusing Components Across the Application

Well-designed components don't just do one thing—they do one thing well and make it easy for other parts of the application to use them. A reusable component should:

Accept data through `@Input()` so it's flexible.

Emit events using `@Output()` so it's interactive.

Avoid coupling to specific services or hardcoded logic unless explicitly needed.

For example, you might create a `NotificationComponent` that displays messages:

```
@Component({
  selector: 'app-notification',
  standalone: true,
  template: `
    <div class="notification" *ngIf="visible">
      {{ message }}
      <button (click)="close()">×</button>
    </div>
  `,
  styles: [`
    .notification { background: #eef; padding:
12px; margin: 10px 0; }
  `]
})
export class NotificationComponent {
  @Input() message = '';
  @Input() visible = true;
  @Output() closed = new EventEmitter<void>();

  close() {
    this.closed.emit();
  }
}
```

Now you can reuse this in any context, for any message:

```
<app-notification

  [message]="'Saved successfully!'"

  [visible]="isVisible"

  (closed)="isVisible = false"

></app-notification>
```

The component doesn't know or care what context it's in—it simply receives its inputs and emits an output when it's closed. That's reusability in action.

Communicating Between Sibling Components

While parent-child communication is direct and encouraged, sibling-to-sibling communication is more indirect. In Angular, siblings should communicate through a shared parent or through a shared service with RxJS or Signals.

Suppose you have a form component and a preview component. Both are children of a parent component. When the user types into the form, the preview should update in real time.

Use the parent as the single source of truth:

Parent component:

```
export class EditorComponent {

  content = '';

}
```

Template:

```
<app-editor-form [(content)]="content"></app-editor-form>

<app-preview [content]="content"></app-preview>
```

The form uses `[(content)]` to bind two-way to the parent, and the preview receives updates through `[content]`.

This design keeps data centralized and consistent, which simplifies debugging and ensures reactivity.

Avoiding Tight Coupling

Component communication is most effective when components remain loosely coupled. Avoid having child components call methods on the parent directly or inject services that belong to higher layers of the app. Use `@Input` and `@Output` for anything involving UI interaction. Use shared services for global coordination or cross-feature communication.

A well-structured Angular application favors composition over inheritance. You build new features by combining existing components rather than extending them or rewriting logic.

For example, a `ProductTileComponent` can be reused in a product listing page, a search result page, and a shopping cart—just by passing different inputs. Its layout stays consistent, but its behavior adapts to context via configuration and event handling.

Component communication is at the core of building robust Angular applications. When you treat each component as an independent unit that knows how to receive data and signal events outward, you're creating building blocks that scale across your application. This encourages a clean separation of concerns, prevents unintentional dependencies, and makes your UI logic easier to reason about.

Chapter 4: Managing State and Forms

User interaction is at the heart of every application. Whether you're building a simple contact form, a signup flow, or a multi-step wizard, capturing and managing user input reliably is essential. Angular provides two powerful ways to handle forms—**template-driven** and **reactive forms**—each with distinct strengths.

Alongside forms, managing **state** becomes critical as your application grows. You need to track what the user is doing, what the app should display, what has been submitted, and what errors need to be shown. In Angular 19.2, the introduction of **Signals** makes state management cleaner and more performant. And when you need state to persist or be shared across components, **services** come into play.

Template-Driven and Reactive Forms

Angular gives you two robust approaches to handle user input through forms: **template-driven forms** and **reactive forms**. Both are part of Angular's core capabilities, and both can handle validation, submission, and data binding. But they serve different needs, and understanding how they differ—along with when to use each—is essential for writing forms that are maintainable, predictable, and scalable.

The choice between template-driven and reactive forms comes down to how much control you need over your form's structure and behavior. In this section, you'll not only see how each method works, but also understand how Angular manages form states under the hood and how to apply these techniques in real applications.

Template-Driven Forms: Simplicity Through Declarative HTML

Template-driven forms put the focus on the HTML template. You describe your form's structure and logic directly in the markup using Angular directives such as `ngModel`, `ngForm`, and form-related attributes. This approach is more declarative and is especially suitable when working with simple forms that don't require complex logic, dynamic structure, or nested control manipulation.

Let's walk through a simple contact form using the template-driven approach.

Component class:

```
export class ContactFormComponent {
  name: string = '';
  email: string = '';
  message: string = '';

  submitForm() {
    console.log({
      name: this.name,
      email: this.email,
      message: this.message
    });
  }
}
```

Template:

```
<form #contactForm="ngForm"
(ngSubmit)="submitForm()">
  <label>
    Name:
    <input name="name" [(ngModel)]="name" required
/>
  </label>

  <label>
    Email:
    <input name="email" [(ngModel)]="email"
required email />
  </label>

  <label>
    Message:
    <textarea name="message" [(ngModel)]="message"
required></textarea>
  </label>

  <button type="submit"
[disabled]="contactForm.invalid">Send</button>
</form>
```

Here's what's happening:

`ngModel` establishes two-way binding between form fields and component properties.

The form is assigned a local template reference variable `#contactForm="ngForm"`, which gives access to the form's status and validation state.

`ngSubmit` binds to a method in the component and triggers on form submission.

Angular handles form state and validation behind the scenes using the DOM structure and directives. The simplicity is great for quick development and clear markup. However, when your form logic becomes more dynamic—adding fields conditionally, responding to control changes, resetting values programmatically—template-driven forms start to feel limited.

Reactive Forms: Explicit Control in the Component Class

Reactive forms give you full control over your form structure and behavior by moving the definition of the form into the component class. You explicitly construct a `FormGroup` and define each `FormControl` programmatically, then bind them to the template using directives like `formGroup` and `formControlName`.

Let's recreate the same contact form using a reactive approach.

Component class:

```
import { Component } from '@angular/core';
import { FormBuilder, FormGroup, Validators } from
'@angular/forms';

@Component({
  selector: 'app-contact-form',
  templateUrl: './contact-form.component.html'
})
export class ContactFormComponent {
  contactForm: FormGroup;

  constructor(private fb: FormBuilder) {
```

```
      this.contactForm = this.fb.group({
        name: ['', Validators.required],
        email: ['', [Validators.required,
Validators.email]],
        message: ['', Validators.required]
      });
  }

  submitForm() {
    if (this.contactForm.valid) {
      console.log(this.contactForm.value);
    }
  }
}
```

Template:

```
<form [formGroup]="contactForm"
(ngSubmit)="submitForm()">
  <label>
    Name:
    <input formControlName="name" />
  </label>

  <label>
    Email:
    <input formControlName="email" />
  </label>

  <label>
    Message:
    <textarea formControlName="message"></textarea>
  </label>

  <button type="submit"
[disabled]="contactForm.invalid">Send</button>
</form>
```

With reactive forms:

The form's structure is defined in code. You can clearly see all validators, default values, and control configuration in one place.

Validators are applied directly at the time of control creation.

The form state (`valid`, `dirty`, `touched`, etc.) is explicitly available in the component and easily testable.

You can subscribe to value changes, dynamically add/remove controls, and reset values programmatically without relying on DOM references.

This approach is well-suited for forms that:

Have dynamic structure (such as adding/removing controls at runtime)

Require complex validation logic or custom validation

Need tight integration with other component logic or services

Are reused or tested as standalone units

Feature Comparison and Real-World Guidance

Both approaches are integrated into Angular's core and share many underlying mechanisms—like form state tracking and validation handling—but their usage models differ significantly.

Here's a real-world scenario to help understand when each form type makes sense:

Suppose you're building a job application form:

A basic form with a few required fields like name, email, and a message? Template-driven will serve you well. It's quick to build and readable directly from the template.

A multi-step form that includes conditional fields, backend validation, file uploads, and dynamic section generation? Use reactive forms. You'll have the programmatic control necessary to manage these complexities efficiently.

Also, remember that Angular allows you to **mix both approaches**. You might use template-driven forms for simple pages and reactive forms in more advanced components, depending on what's needed.

For consistency and long-term maintainability in large codebases, reactive forms are often the preferred choice, especially in enterprise-grade applications.

Both template-driven and reactive forms are powerful, but they serve different design needs. Angular empowers you to choose based on the nature of your project, the complexity of your UI, and how much control you want in your component code. When used thoughtfully, both form styles allow you to build responsive, validated, and reliable input systems with ease.

Validation Strategies and Custom Validators

Handling form validation correctly is critical to both user experience and data integrity. Whether you're collecting a simple contact message or building a multi-step registration workflow, users need immediate, clear feedback about what's valid and what isn't—and your backend should only receive clean, well-structured data. Angular gives you two tightly integrated tools to do this: **built-in validators** and **custom validators**. Both work in template-driven and reactive forms, but how you apply them and how much control you need will influence your implementation.

Using Angular's Built-in Validators

Angular provides several built-in validators that cover the most common validation cases:

`required`

`minlength` / `maxlength`

`pattern`

`email`

When you're using **template-driven forms**, these are added directly to the input fields as HTML attributes:

```
<form #form="ngForm" (ngSubmit)="submit()">
  <input name="email" ngModel required email />
  <div *ngIf="form.submitted &&
form.controls['email']?.errors?.['required']">
    Email is required.
  </div>
  <div *ngIf="form.submitted &&
form.controls['email']?.errors?.['email']">
    Invalid email address.
```

```
    </div>
</form>
```

Angular automatically picks up on these attributes and tracks form validity. The `errors` property on a control contains a map of which validation rules failed.

In **reactive forms**, validators are passed programmatically when you define your form controls:

```
import { Validators, FormBuilder } from
'@angular/forms';


this.registrationForm = this.fb.group({

  email: ['', [Validators.required,
Validators.email]],

  password: ['', [Validators.required,
Validators.minLength(6)]]

});
```

To show validation errors in the template, you access the form control and its error state:

```
<input formControlName="password" />
<div
*ngIf="registrationForm.get('password')?.errors?.['
required']">
  Password is required.
</div>
<div
*ngIf="registrationForm.get('password')?.errors?.['
minlength']">
  Password must be at least 6 characters.
</div>
```

These validators provide immediate value with minimal effort. But sometimes, your logic goes beyond what built-in rules can express. That's where custom validators come in.

Writing Synchronous Custom Validators

A **synchronous custom validator** is a simple function that returns either `null` (when valid) or an object with error details (when invalid). This function runs during form evaluation and integrates with Angular's validation mechanism.

Suppose you want to prevent usernames that include spaces. You could write a validator like this:

```
import { AbstractControl, ValidationErrors } from
'@angular/forms';

export function noSpaces(control: AbstractControl):
ValidationErrors | null {
  const hasSpace = (control.value || '').includes('
');
  return hasSpace ? { noSpaces: true } : null;
}
```

Apply it when defining a control:

```
this.signupForm = this.fb.group({

  username: ['', [Validators.required, noSpaces]]

});
```

And in the template:

```
<div
*ngIf="signupForm.get('username')?.errors?.['noSpac
es']">

  Username cannot contain spaces.

</div>
```

You can also include parameters in your validator. Let's say you want to enforce a minimum numeric value:

```
export function minValue(min: number) {
  return (control: AbstractControl):
ValidationErrors | null => {
```

```
    const value = +control.value;
    return isNaN(value) || value < min ? {
minValue: { requiredMin: min } } : null;
   };
}
```
Usage:
```
this.orderForm = this.fb.group({
  quantity: [1, [minValue(5)]]
});
```

This flexibility lets you define validation rules that precisely match your application's logic.

Writing Asynchronous Custom Validators

Some validations can't be done immediately—they require backend communication. A common example is checking whether a username or email is already taken.

An **asynchronous validator** returns an `Observable` that emits `null` if valid, or a validation error object if invalid.

Let's create a mock async validator that checks if a username is taken:

```
import { AbstractControl, ValidationErrors } from
'@angular/forms';
import { Observable, of } from 'rxjs';
import { delay, map } from 'rxjs/operators';

export function usernameTaken(control:
AbstractControl): Observable<ValidationErrors |
null> {
  const forbiddenUsernames = ['admin', 'root',
'test'];
  const username = control.value;

  return
of(forbiddenUsernames.includes(username)).pipe(
    delay(300),
    map(isTaken => (isTaken ? { usernameTaken: true
} : null))
  );
}
```

Apply it like this:

```
this.signupForm = this.fb.group({
  username: ['', {
    validators: [Validators.required],
    asyncValidators: [usernameTaken],
    updateOn: 'blur'
  }]
});
```

Note the `updateOn: 'blur'` setting—it delays validation until the user leaves the input field. This is important for performance when validators involve API calls.

Template feedback:

```
<div *ngIf="signupForm.get('username')?.pending">
  Checking username availability...
</div>
<div
*ngIf="signupForm.get('username')?.errors?.['userna
meTaken']">
  That username is already taken.
</div>
```

For production-ready forms, you would typically call your backend using `HttpClient` inside the validator. The async validator pattern remains the same—only the Observable source changes.

Cross-Field Validation

Sometimes, you need to validate multiple controls together. A common case is **password confirmation**. In this case, validation needs access to multiple controls inside a `FormGroup`.

Here's how you might write a group-level validator:

```
export function passwordMatch(group:
AbstractControl): ValidationErrors | null {
  const password = group.get('password')?.value;
  const confirm =
group.get('confirmPassword')?.value;
```

```
  return password === confirm ? null : {
passwordMismatch: true };
}
```

Usage:

```
this.form = this.fb.group({

  password: ['', Validators.required],

  confirmPassword: ['', Validators.required]

}, { validators: passwordMatch });
```

Then in the template:

```
<div *ngIf="form.errors?.['passwordMismatch']">

  Passwords do not match.

</div>
```

Group-level validators are essential when your validation logic spans more than one field.

Responding to Validation State in the UI

Whether you're using built-in or custom validators, the goal is to give users immediate, helpful feedback. Angular exposes several control state properties for this:

`touched`: the user has focused and blurred the field

`dirty`: the field's value has changed

`valid`/`invalid`: whether the control passed all validators

`pending`: if an async validator is running

A good rule of thumb is to show error messages **only when the control has been touched or the form has been submitted**. This avoids overwhelming users with errors before they've interacted with the form.

Example:

```
<div *ngIf="emailControl.invalid &&
(emailControl.dirty || emailControl.touched)">
  <small
*ngIf="emailControl.errors?.['required']">Email is
required.</small>
  <small
*ngIf="emailControl.errors?.['email']">Email format
is invalid.</small>
</div>
```

This gives users feedback only when it's helpful—and not before.

Validation in Angular is comprehensive and flexible. With built-in validators, you can cover the basics quickly. With custom synchronous and asynchronous validators, you can implement the unique rules your application demands. And by combining form states and reactive logic, you can build forms that are user-friendly, consistent, and secure.

Working with Signals for State Handling

In Angular 19.2, **Signals** provide a modern, efficient, and more controlled way to manage local component state. This new reactivity model offers a clearer, more granular alternative to Angular's traditional change detection based on `Zone.js`. With Signals, your component state becomes more predictable, easier to reason about, and more efficient to update—especially in performance-sensitive or interactive applications.

Angular's implementation of Signals is inspired by reactive primitives used in frameworks like Solid and Svelte, but it's tailored for Angular's architecture and integrates natively with templates, forms, lifecycle hooks, and change detection.

Understanding the Signal Primitive

A Signal in Angular is a container for a reactive value. You **read** a Signal by calling it as a function, and you **update** it using `.set()` or `.update()` methods. Unlike observables or subjects, Signals are **synchronous**, **push-based**, and **automatically tracked** by the Angular rendering engine.

Let's create a basic Signal to track a counter:

```
import { signal } from '@angular/core';
```

```
export class CounterComponent {
  count = signal(0);

  increment() {
    this.count.set(this.count() + 1);
  }
}
```

To **read** the current value of the Signal, you call it like a function:

```
<p>Count: {{ count() }}</p>
```

Every time `count.set()` is called, Angular updates the DOM—but only the DOM elements that depend on `count()`. This is what makes Signals more efficient: Angular doesn't run change detection across the whole component tree. It updates only what's necessary.

If you want to **modify** a Signal's value relative to its current value, use `.update()`:

```
decrement() {

  this.count.update(n => n - 1);

}
```

This guarantees that you're working with the latest value and avoids race conditions.

Deriving State with Computed Signals

Sometimes you need values that are **based on other Signals**—but you don't want to manually update them whenever the source changes. This is what `computed()` is for. A computed Signal automatically recalculates whenever any of its dependencies change.

For example:

```
import { computed } from '@angular/core';

export class CounterComponent {
  count = signal(2);
```

```
  doubled = computed(() => this.count() * 2);
}
```

In the template:

```
<p>Original: {{ count() }}</p>

<p>Doubled: {{ doubled() }}</p>
```

Angular tracks the dependency between `doubled` and `count` internally. When `count` changes, `doubled` automatically recomputes. You don't need to manage subscriptions, lifecycle hooks, or manual updates.

This model leads to more declarative and predictable code.

Triggering Side Effects with `effect()`

While Signals are great for expressing reactive state, sometimes you need to perform side effects—logging to the console, updating local storage, or triggering navigation. Use `effect()` to do this safely in response to Signal changes.

Here's how you might track analytics when a user visits a section of your app:

```
import { effect, signal } from '@angular/core';

export class PageTrackerComponent {
  currentPage = signal('home');

  constructor() {
    effect(() => {
      console.log(`User navigated to:
${this.currentPage()}`);
    });
  }

  goToPage(page: string) {
    this.currentPage.set(page);
  }
}
```

Whenever `currentPage()` changes, the `effect()` function runs automatically. You don't have to manually subscribe or clean up—it integrates with Angular's lifecycle and unmounts safely when the component is destroyed.

For example, you might use `effect()` to update the page title:

```
effect(() => {

  document.title = `Viewing:
${this.currentPage()}`;

});
```

This keeps your logic tightly coupled to the state that drives it, without side effects leaking into other parts of your code.

Using Signals in the Template

Signals integrate seamlessly into Angular templates. Any time you use `{{ signal() }}` in a template or bind a Signal's value in an attribute, Angular automatically tracks that dependency and updates the DOM efficiently.

```
<h1>Welcome, {{ userName() }}</h1>

<button (click)="changeName()">Change Name</button>
```

In the component:

```
userName = signal('Ada');



changeName() {

  this.userName.set('Grace');

}
```

Angular's rendering engine knows that this binding depends on `userName()` and will re-render this specific part of the DOM when it changes—no need to trigger change detection manually.

Combining Signals with Forms

Although Angular's forms system was originally built around `FormControl`, Signals work well as a complementary mechanism for tracking reactive form-like state, especially when you're working with UI logic that doesn't need the full weight of `FormGroup`.

Here's a simple use case using Signals to manage form input:

```
export class FeedbackComponent {
  message = signal('');
  submitted = signal(false);

  submit() {
    if (this.message().trim()) {
      this.submitted.set(true);
    }
  }

  reset() {
    this.message.set('');
    this.submitted.set(false);
  }
}
```

Template:

```
<form (submit)="submit(); $event.preventDefault()">

  <textarea [(ngModel)]="message()"></textarea>

  <button type="submit">Send</button>

</form>



<p *ngIf="submitted()">Thanks for your feedback!</p>
```

You can even wire this up to disable the submit button based on computed validity:

```
readonly canSubmit = computed(() =>
this.message().trim().length > 0);
```

```
<button type="submit"
[disabled]="!canSubmit()">Send</button>
```

This approach is lightweight and declarative—perfect for simple UIs or when working outside of Angular's full reactive forms API.

Creating Signal-Based Services

You can use Signals inside Angular services just like you would in a component. This is useful when you want to share reactive state across multiple parts of your application.

Here's an example of a simple cart service:

```
import { Injectable, signal, computed } from
'@angular/core';

@Injectable({ providedIn: 'root' })
export class CartService {
  private items = signal<{ name: string; quantity:
number }[]>([]);

  readonly totalItems = computed(() =>
    this.items().reduce((sum, item) => sum +
item.quantity, 0)
  );

  addItem(name: string, quantity = 1) {
    const updated = [...this.items()];
    const existing = updated.find(i => i.name ===
name);

    if (existing) {
      existing.quantity += quantity;
    } else {
      updated.push({ name, quantity });
    }

    this.items.set(updated);
  }

  getItems() {
    return this.items();
```

```
    }
}
```

In your component:

```
constructor(public cart: CartService) {}

<p>Total items: {{ cart.totalItems() }}</p>
```

This makes it easy to track and react to application state from any component. You avoid RxJS boilerplate and gain clear, direct state flow with reactive updates.

When to Use Signals Over RxJS

Use Signals when:

You're managing local or UI-specific state.

You want automatic dependency tracking in the DOM.

You need reactivity that's easy to test and reason about.

You're optimizing for performance in rendering-heavy apps.

Use RxJS when:

You're dealing with streams of events over time (e.g., websocket, timers).

You need cancellation, mapping, and composition operators.

You're integrating with Angular's `HttpClient`, `Router`, or `FormControl`.

They're not mutually exclusive. In fact, Angular provides tools to bridge both systems: `fromObservable` and `toObservable()` allow interoperability between Signals and observables.

Signals represent a shift toward **more predictable, component-driven state management** in Angular. They reduce overhead, remove the need for manual subscriptions or change detection triggers, and improve both code clarity and performance.

Organizing State with Local and Shared Services

Managing state in Angular goes beyond just setting and reading variables. As your application scales, state begins to span across multiple components and features. At that point, you'll need a strategy to ensure consistency, reduce duplication, and maintain clean separation between components and the logic that powers them. Angular gives you a clear solution for this: **services**.

Services allow you to encapsulate and share state. Whether you're tracking UI-specific variables like form visibility, application-level concerns like authentication status, or business data like a shopping cart or form wizard steps, organizing state through services is a foundational practice.

Angular 19.2 enhances this further with **Signals**, allowing you to manage state reactively within services—without resorting to complex observable chains or manual change detection.

When to Keep State Local

In Angular, a component should manage its own state when:

That state only affects the component itself.

It doesn't need to be shared with siblings or parents.

It's transient—like toggling visibility of a dropdown or tracking form validity within one screen.

For example:

```
import { signal } from '@angular/core';

export class AccordionComponent {
  isOpen = signal(false);

  toggle() {
    this.isOpen.update(value => !value);
  }
}
```

Template:

```
<div (click)="toggle()">
  <h3>Section Title</h3>
</div>
<div *ngIf="isOpen()">Content visible when
open</div>
```

This is clean, isolated state. The component doesn't need a service here.

When and Why to Use Shared Services

When state needs to be accessed by **multiple components**, you should lift it into a shared service. This could mean:

Two sibling components need access to the same data.

A modal or snackbar component needs to respond to user actions across routes.

You need to persist UI state or data between navigation events.

Forms that span across multiple steps or components.

Angular services are perfect for this because they're singletons by default and injected using Angular's dependency injection system. They exist independently of the component tree and outlive components unless scoped explicitly.

Here's how to set up a shared service using Signals for application-wide notification state.

Example: Notification Service with Signals

Service:
```
import { Injectable, signal, effect } from
'@angular/core';

@Injectable({ providedIn: 'root' })
export class NotificationService {
  private _message = signal<string | null>(null);
  readonly message = this._message.asReadonly();

  show(message: string, timeout: number = 3000) {
    this._message.set(message);
```

```
    setTimeout(() => {
       this.clear();
    }, timeout);
  }

  clear() {
    this._message.set(null);
  }
}
```

In this service:

`signal` stores the message value.

`.asReadonly()` exposes a read-only version of the signal to prevent external mutation.

A timeout auto-clears the message after a short duration.

Now in your `NotificationComponent`:

```
export class NotificationComponent {

   constructor(public notify: NotificationService)
{}

}
```

Template:

```
<div *ngIf="notify.message() as msg" class="toast">

   {{ msg }}
</div>
```

This `NotificationComponent` can be placed in your root layout. Any other component in the app can now trigger a message:

```
this.notify.show('Settings saved');
```

The state is now cleanly centralized. No manual DOM manipulation, no tight coupling, no shared mutable variables.

Example: Multi-Step Form State in a Service

Let's say you're building a registration wizard split across three components: StepOneComponent, StepTwoComponent, and StepThreeComponent.

Create a RegistrationService to store and coordinate shared form state:

```
import { Injectable, signal } from '@angular/core';

interface RegistrationData {
  name?: string;
  email?: string;
  password?: string;
}

@Injectable({ providedIn: 'root' })
export class RegistrationService {
  private _step = signal(1);
  private _data = signal<RegistrationData>({});

  readonly step = this._step.asReadonly();
  readonly data = this._data.asReadonly();

  nextStep() {
    this._step.set(this._step() + 1);
  }

  prevStep() {
    this._step.set(this._step() - 1);
  }

  update(data: Partial<RegistrationData>) {
    this._data.set({ ...this._data(), ...data });
  }

  reset() {
    this._step.set(1);
    this._data.set({});
  }
}
```

In `StepOneComponent`, update user details:

```
export class StepOneComponent {
  name = signal('');

  constructor(private reg: RegistrationService) {}

  next() {
    this.reg.update({ name: this.name() });
    this.reg.nextStep();
  }
}
```

In `StepTwoComponent`, read previous data:

```
export class StepTwoComponent {
  constructor(public reg: RegistrationService) {}

  get email() {
    return this.reg.data().email || '';
  }
}
```

Your shared service now holds a reactive, centralized form state across components—without manual event emitters, `@Input/@Output` chains, or global stores.

Benefits of Using Signals in Services

Synchronous and Predictable – Signals update immediately and trigger only what's needed.

Encapsulation – Expose `readonly` signals from your service to maintain clear separation between the internal logic and consuming components.

No Subscriptions – Unlike observables or subjects, there's no `.subscribe()`/`.unsubscribe()` lifecycle management.

Template Friendly – Signals bind directly into templates using `()`, updating DOM efficiently and automatically.

This model encourages creating services that are focused, self-contained, and composable. You can even compose one service into another, using Signals as reactive state boundaries.

Testing State in Services

Testing services that use Signals is straightforward because they're deterministic and synchronous.

```
it('should update message', () => {
  const service = new NotificationService();
  service.show('Test');

  expect(service.message()).toBe('Test');
});
```

No fakeAsync or timers unless you're testing time-based logic. Signals give you confidence that your business logic works as expected without mock subscriptions or zones.

Angular encourages modularity. By moving shared or cross-cutting state into injectable services and tracking it with Signals, you avoid fragile component inter-dependencies. You keep logic where it belongs—inside services—and keep your components focused on presentation.

Chapter 5: Navigation and Routing Architecture

Routing is what turns your Angular application from a simple component shell into a full single-page application. It's the system that maps URLs to views, loads modules dynamically, controls access to routes, passes data between components, and drives the overall structure of your app.

Angular's Router is feature-rich and designed to handle everything from simple page navigation to complex, nested layouts, lazy-loaded feature modules, and secure route access. In this chapter, you'll learn not just the syntax of routes—but how to use routing to architect scalable, maintainable, and performant applications.

Angular Router Basics

Routing in Angular enables you to map specific URLs to components. It's how you create true single-page applications (SPAs), where the user navigates between pages without reloading the browser. When routing is set up properly, your application feels seamless, fast, and logically structured. And with Angular 19.2, especially when using standalone components, the routing setup becomes even more streamlined.

Configuring Routes in Angular

The Router is provided by the `@angular/router` package. Before you can use it, you need to define a **route configuration**, which is simply an array of route objects, each describing a path and the component that should be displayed when that path is active.

Here's a basic example of a route configuration:

```
import { Routes } from '@angular/router';
import { HomeComponent } from './home.component';
import { AboutComponent } from './about.component';

export const routes: Routes = [
  { path: '', component: HomeComponent },
  { path: 'about', component: AboutComponent }
];
```

Each object in the array maps a `path` to a `component`. The empty string `''` is the default route (root URL `/`). Now when the user visits `/about`, Angular displays `AboutComponent`. When they visit `/`, it shows `HomeComponent`.

To activate the router and apply these routes to your app, you need to register them using Angular's `provideRouter()` function.

For standalone apps in Angular 19.2, this is usually done during bootstrap:

```
import { bootstrapApplication } from
'@angular/platform-browser';

import { AppComponent } from './app.component';

import { provideRouter } from '@angular/router';

import { routes } from './app.routes';


bootstrapApplication(AppComponent, {

  providers: [provideRouter(routes)]

});
```

With this setup, your app is now router-aware.

Displaying Routed Views with `<router-outlet>`

After defining routes, you need to tell Angular where to insert the routed component. This is done using the `<router-outlet>` directive in your root component template:

`<router-outlet></router-outlet>`

This tag acts like a dynamic container. Whenever the URL changes, Angular determines which component matches the route and injects it into the router outlet.

Here's how it works:

Visiting `/` loads `HomeComponent`

Visiting `/about` loads `AboutComponent`

This routing logic is fully dynamic and managed by Angular based on your `routes` configuration.

Navigating Between Routes with `routerLink`

You don't need to use raw anchor (`<a href>`) tags to navigate. Angular provides a directive called `routerLink`, which generates the correct URL and updates the browser's history without triggering a full page reload.

Example:

```
<nav>
  <a routerLink="/">Home</a>
  <a routerLink="/about">About</a>
</nav>
```

When clicked, Angular updates the URL and loads the correct component inside the router outlet.

You can also bind a route programmatically:

```
<button [routerLink]="['/about']">Go to
About</button>
```

Or for navigation with parameters:

```
this.router.navigate(['/product', 42]);
```

To use the `navigate` function, inject Angular's `Router` service:

```
import { Router } from '@angular/router';

constructor(private router: Router) {}
```

This method gives you more control—such as passing dynamic values, conditionally routing, or building URLs based on app logic.

Using Route Parameters

Sometimes you need to pass dynamic values through the URL—for example, displaying a specific product or user by ID. Angular supports route parameters using the colon syntax in the path definition.

Define a route with a parameter:

```
{ path: 'product/:id', component: ProductComponent
}
```

Now if a user navigates to `/product/15`, Angular loads `ProductComponent` and makes `15` available as a parameter.

In your component, you access this parameter by injecting `ActivatedRoute`:

```
import { ActivatedRoute } from '@angular/router';

export class ProductComponent {
  constructor(private route: ActivatedRoute) {}

  ngOnInit() {
    const id =
this.route.snapshot.paramMap.get('id');
    console.log('Product ID:', id);
  }
}
```

Alternatively, if you want to react to changes over time (such as when the route changes but the component stays mounted), you can subscribe to the parameter observable:

```
this.route.paramMap.subscribe(params => {

  const id = params.get('id');

});
```

This is particularly useful for components that stay alive while the route changes, like tabbed layouts or dashboards.

Wildcard and Fallback Routes

To handle unknown routes or create a "Not Found" page, define a wildcard route using `**`:

```
{ path: '**', component: NotFoundComponent }
```

Place this route **last** in the routes array—Angular matches routes in the order they are declared, and the wildcard will catch any paths not handled by earlier routes.

This is how you protect your app from broken URLs or unexpected navigation patterns.

Redirecting Routes

You can redirect one path to another using `redirectTo`:

```
{ path: 'home', redirectTo: '', pathMatch: 'full' }
```

This tells Angular that when the user navigates to `/home`, it should redirect to `/`.

The `pathMatch: 'full'` is critical—it tells Angular to match the **whole** path. Without it, Angular might redirect unintentionally on partial matches.

The Angular Router isn't just a tool for changing views. It's a foundational part of how Angular apps are structured. From the very start, it controls how your app responds to URLs, how components are shown or hidden, how data is passed between pages, and how users interact with different sections.

Whether you're working with simple navigation menus or building an enterprise-grade application with deeply nested feature modules, the principles remain the same: define clear routes, use router outlets for display, navigate with `routerLink` or `navigate()`, and manage parameters in a predictable, type-safe way.

Route Guards, Lazy Loading, and Named Outlets

In real-world Angular applications, routing involves more than mapping URLs to components. You often need to **protect routes**, **optimize loading performance**, and **handle complex layouts** where multiple routed views appear on the same screen. Angular equips you with three essential tools for these challenges: **route guards**, **lazy loading**, and **named outlets**. Used properly, they allow you to design secure, responsive, and maintainable routing systems that scale with your application.

Route Guards: Controlling Access to Routes

Angular route guards give you control over whether a user can access a particular route. These are especially useful when implementing authentication, authorization, or conditional navigation. Guards are simply functions or services that return a boolean, a URL redirect, or an observable/promise that resolves to either of those.

There are different guard types, each with a distinct purpose:

CanActivate: checks if a route can be entered.

CanDeactivate: checks if the user can leave a route/component.

CanActivateChild: used for nested routes.

Resolve: pre-fetches data before loading a route.

CanLoad: used to prevent lazy-loaded modules from being loaded.

Creating a Basic CanActivate Guard

Let's say you want to prevent unauthenticated users from accessing a dashboard.

Create the guard function:

```
import { CanActivateFn } from '@angular/router';
import { inject } from '@angular/core';
import { AuthService } from './auth.service';

export const authGuard: CanActivateFn = () => {
  const auth = inject(AuthService);
  return auth.isLoggedIn(); // returns true or
false
};
```

In your route definition:

```
{ path: 'dashboard', component: DashboardComponent,
canActivate: [authGuard] }
```

This guard will prevent access unless isLoggedIn() returns true. If you want to redirect unauthenticated users to /login, modify the guard like this:

```
import { Router } from '@angular/router';

export const authGuard: CanActivateFn = () => {
  const auth = inject(AuthService);
  const router = inject(Router);

  if (!auth.isLoggedIn()) {
    router.navigate(['/login']);
    return false;
  }

  return true;
};
```

This approach is fully synchronous. If you need to wait on asynchronous data (like verifying a token or calling an API), you can return an observable or promise:

```
return auth.checkTokenValidity().pipe(

  map(isValid => isValid ||
router.createUrlTree(['/login']))

);
```

Lazy Loading: Improve Performance with On-Demand Routing

Lazy loading helps your Angular app load faster by only loading feature modules or components when they're needed. Instead of bundling your entire app into one JavaScript file, Angular separates it into **chunks** and loads them on demand.

Lazy Loading Standalone Components

With standalone components in Angular 19.2, lazy loading is simpler and more flexible.

Suppose you have a settings page that should be loaded only when the user visits /settings.

Define the route:

```
{ path: 'settings', loadComponent: () =>
import('./settings/settings.component').then(m =>
m.SettingsComponent) }
```

Now when the user navigates to /settings, Angular dynamically imports and renders the component. Until then, it's not included in the main bundle—saving bandwidth and speeding up the initial load.

Lazy Loading a Feature Module

If you're still using module-based architecture (for example, for backward compatibility or grouping routes), you can lazy load an entire module:

```
{ path: 'admin', loadChildren: () =>
import('./admin/admin.routes').then(m =>
m.ADMIN_ROUTES) }
```

This setup allows an entire section of your app—including its routes, components, and services—to be isolated and lazy-loaded when needed.

Lazy loading is particularly valuable in large applications where initial load time is critical. Sections like dashboards, reports, admin areas, and feature-heavy modals are good candidates for lazy loading.

Named Outlets: Display Multiple Routed Views Simultaneously

In many applications, you might want to show multiple routed views on the same screen. For example, a main content area and a sidebar that each loads independently based on route changes. Angular supports this through **named outlets**.

By default, Angular uses a single unnamed <router-outlet>, which handles your primary view. To show more than one routed view at a time, define additional <router-outlet name="xyz"> elements in your template and assign routes to them using the outlet property.

Setup Example

Template:

```
<router-outlet></router-outlet> <!-- primary view -
->
```

```
<router-outlet name="sidebar"></router-outlet> <!--
named outlet -->
```

Routes:

```
const routes: Routes = [
  { path: '', component: HomeComponent },
  {
    path: 'help',
    component: HelpSidebarComponent,
    outlet: 'sidebar'
  }
];
```

To activate a named outlet from code:

```
this.router.navigate([{ outlets: { sidebar:
['help'] } }]);
```

To close the outlet:

```
this.router.navigate([{ outlets: { sidebar: null }
}]);
```

You can also construct links declaratively:

```
<a [routerLink]="[{ outlets: { sidebar: ['help'] }
}]">Open Help</a>
```

Named outlets are extremely useful when:

You have floating panels (like modals, drawers, or sidebars).

You want to preserve a primary view while loading secondary routed content.

You need multiple parallel navigation paths in the same layout.

Real-World Combination

In a typical enterprise dashboard:

You lazy load the reports module under /reports.

You protect it with canActivate to ensure only admins access it.

You use a named outlet called `sidebar` to open a feedback panel or help widget.

Example route definitions:

```
{
  path: 'reports',
  loadChildren: () =>
import('./reports/reports.routes').then(m =>
m.REPORTS_ROUTES),
  canActivate: [adminGuard]
},
{
  path: 'feedback',
  component: FeedbackPanelComponent,
  outlet: 'sidebar'
}
```

This gives you a clean, scalable, and user-friendly app architecture.

Using **route guards**, **lazy loading**, and **named outlets** allows you to design navigation systems that are secure, efficient, and flexible:

Guards protect sensitive routes and ensure user permissions are enforced.

Lazy loading trims your initial bundle and accelerates startup performance.

Named outlets enable multi-pane navigation and dynamic view composition.

These features are foundational to writing production-quality Angular applications. They go beyond routing for display—they shape how users move through your app, how your code is structured, and how you deliver performance and control at scale.

Advanced Routing Techniques in Angular 19.2

Angular 19.2 brings refinements to its router that align with its push toward standalone components, fine-grained reactivity with Signals, and modular application design. While the basics of routing—mapping paths to components—remain familiar, the advanced features in 19.2 provide more precise control over route composition, data binding, and dependency scoping.

Binding Route Parameters to Component Inputs

One of the most ergonomic improvements in Angular 19.2 is the ability to automatically bind **route parameters** to component @Input() properties. This replaces the need for manually injecting ActivatedRoute and parsing parameters with .snapshot or .paramMap.

Here's how it works.

Let's say you have a route like this:

```
{ path: 'user/:id', component:
UserProfileComponent, data: { inputs: ['id'] } }
```

And your standalone component:

```
import { Component, Input } from '@angular/core';

@Component({
  selector: 'app-user-profile',
  standalone: true,
  template: `<p>Viewing user ID: {{ id }}</p>`
})
export class UserProfileComponent {
  @Input() id!: string;
}
```

Angular now binds the :id from the URL directly to the @Input() without any boilerplate. If the user navigates to /user/45, id will be '45'.

This feature works for:

Route **parameters** (e.g., :id)

Route **query parameters**

Route **data** (provided via data property in the route config)

It reduces code complexity, especially in stateless presentation components.

Route-Level Dependency Providers

Angular 19.2 also allows you to define **providers** directly on a route definition. This means services can be scoped specifically to the lifecycle of a route and automatically cleaned up when the route is deactivated.

Define a service per route:

```
{

  path: 'reports',

  component: ReportsComponent,

  providers: [ReportsService]

}
```

This does three things:

Limits ReportsService to only this route.

Ensures that the instance is destroyed when navigating away.

Avoids polluting the global injector with feature-specific services.

This is extremely useful when:

You want to reuse a service across multiple routes, each with their own isolated state.

You're working with route-specific resources like paginated data or component-scoped caches.

If ReportsService is injected in ReportsComponent or any of its children, Angular automatically resolves it from this local scope.

You can also use route-level providers with **standalone routed feature modules** or **lazy-loaded components**, making them ideal for building self-contained application slices.

Dynamic Route Data with inject()

Instead of accessing route data and parameters through ActivatedRoute, Angular 19.2 allows you to directly inject route state using inject().

This makes your components cleaner and lets you co-locate route-related logic with your reactive setup.

```
import { inject } from '@angular/core';
import { ActivatedRoute } from '@angular/router';

const route = inject(ActivatedRoute);
const id = route.snapshot.paramMap.get('id');
```

Even better, you can use Signals to track route changes reactively.

Using Signals to React to Route Changes

Let's say you want to respond to route parameter changes (e.g., if a user navigates between /user/1 and /user/2 while staying on the same component).

Instead of subscribing to paramMap, you can bind that reactivity into a Signal using computed() or manually updating a signal():

```
import { inject, signal } from '@angular/core';
import { ActivatedRoute } from '@angular/router';

const route = inject(ActivatedRoute);
const userId =
signal(route.snapshot.paramMap.get('id'));

route.paramMap.subscribe(params => {
  userId.set(params.get('id'));
});
```

This setup allows your template to track userId() as a reactive value, and automatically updates when the parameter changes.

Alternatively, you can wrap route observables into a Signal using a utility:

```
import { toSignal } from '@angular/core/rxjs-
interop';

const id$ = route.paramMap.pipe(map(p =>
p.get('id')));
const idSignal = toSignal(id$, { initialValue: null
});
```

This enables you to use reactive route state with Angular's fine-grained change detection and DOM update control.

Combining All Together in a Real Use Case

Let's put all of this into a concrete scenario. You're building a feature for viewing a user's profile by ID, with route-scoped services, direct input binding, and Signal-based tracking.

Your route definition:

```
{
  path: 'profile/:id',
  component: UserComponent,
  data: { inputs: ['id'] },
  providers: [UserService]
}
```

The `UserService` is scoped to this route. It fetches user data based on the ID from the URL.

In `UserComponent`:

```
@Component({
  selector: 'app-user',
  standalone: true,
  template: `
    <div *ngIf="user$() as user">
      <h2>{{ user.name }}</h2>
      <p>Email: {{ user.email }}</p>
    </div>
  `
})
export class UserComponent {
  @Input() id!: string;
  private userService = inject(UserService);
  user$ = signal<User | null>(null);

  ngOnInit() {

this.userService.getUserById(this.id).subscribe(user => {
```

```
        this.user$.set(user);
    });
  }
}
```

This setup:

Reads `id` directly from the URL.

Loads user data using a route-specific service.

Tracks state reactively using a Signal.

Cleans up the service instance automatically when the route is left.

This pattern is robust, clean, and aligned with Angular's standalone and Signals-first direction.

Route Reuse Strategy (Advanced Control)

In some complex applications—especially dashboards—you might want to control whether Angular **reuses a component** when navigating between similar routes, such as `/project/1` and `/project/2`.

Angular supports a custom `RouteReuseStrategy`, but starting in Angular 15+, you can simplify this by using component lifecycle flags.

You can force a component to reload by setting a unique `key` or navigating with a different `routerLink` directive using `[routerLink]` with different `queryParams`.

Alternatively, you can wrap dynamic route reloading logic inside `ngOnChanges` if your `@Input()` values change from route input binding.

Angular 19.2 offers routing features that go beyond simple navigation. With advanced capabilities like:

Binding route params directly to component inputs

Providing services scoped only to the route's lifecycle

Reacting to route state changes with Signals

...you gain more control, less boilerplate, and better structure in your Angular applications. These tools enable more scalable routing patterns and cleaner integration of business logic into view components.

Preloading Strategies for Better UX

When using lazy loading in Angular to split your application into smaller, on-demand chunks, you improve your app's initial load time. But there's a tradeoff: while lazy loading avoids loading unused code, it introduces a delay the first time a user navigates to that route. To solve this, Angular provides **preloading strategies**—mechanisms to fetch lazy-loaded routes **in the background** after your app has booted. This improves perceived performance without sacrificing initial bundle size.

Why Preloading Matters

Without preloading, lazy-loaded modules or components are fetched only when a route is activated. That's okay if the user navigates there infrequently or if network latency is low. But if a feature like `/dashboard` or `/settings` is accessed soon after app load, a delay may occur while Angular fetches the JavaScript chunk and parses it. This often shows up as a flash of blank space, loading spinners, or delayed responsiveness.

Preloading is a smart way to address this. Angular loads routes *after* the initial page is stable—when the browser is idle—so by the time the user clicks a link, the feature is already available.

Using Built-in PreloadAllModules Strategy

Angular offers a built-in strategy called `PreloadAllModules`, which eagerly preloads **all** lazy-loaded routes as soon as possible after the app starts.

To enable it, register your routes with the preloading option:

```
import { provideRouter, withPreloading,
PreloadAllModules } from '@angular/router';
import { routes } from './app.routes';

bootstrapApplication(AppComponent, {
  providers: [provideRouter(routes,
withPreloading(PreloadAllModules))]
});
```

Now all routes that use `loadComponent` or `loadChildren` will be fetched in the background immediately after the app finishes loading.

For example:

```
{ path: 'settings', loadComponent: () =>
import('./settings.component').then(m =>
m.SettingsComponent) }
```

This component will be lazy-loaded, but thanks to preloading, the chunk will be fetched before the user navigates to `/settings`.

This improves responsiveness but can increase bandwidth usage. It's best when:

You have a small number of lazy routes.

Your app is likely to use most routes in a single session.

Users frequently navigate between many screens.

Custom Preloading Strategies

For more control, you can define a **custom strategy** to selectively preload routes based on your own logic—such as route metadata, user role, network status, or usage analytics.

Start by implementing Angular's `PreloadingStrategy` interface:

```
import { Injectable } from '@angular/core';
import { Route, PreloadingStrategy } from
'@angular/router';
import { Observable, of } from 'rxjs';

@Injectable({ providedIn: 'root' })
export class SelectivePreloadStrategy implements
PreloadingStrategy {
  preload(route: Route, load: () =>
Observable<any>): Observable<any> {
    if (route.data?.['preload']) {
      return load(); // load this route
    }
    return of(null); // skip this route
  }
```

```
}
```

This strategy checks for a `data.preload` flag on the route. If present, it preloads the route. Otherwise, it skips it.

Register this strategy:

```
import { provideRouter, withPreloading } from
'@angular/router';

bootstrapApplication(AppComponent, {
  providers: [provideRouter(routes,
withPreloading(SelectivePreloadStrategy))]
});
```

Now annotate routes:

```
{
  path: 'profile',
  loadComponent: () =>
import('./profile.component').then(m =>
m.ProfileComponent),
  data: { preload: true }
}
```

This setup gives you granular control. You can preload only critical routes that users are likely to visit soon—without bloating your app's startup.

Preloading with User Intent and Signals

Sometimes it makes sense to preload a route **just before** a user is likely to access it—such as when they hover over a menu item. You can use Angular's `Router.preload()` method directly to preload a specific route on demand.

Inject the `Router` and use `router.preload()` manually:

```
import { inject } from '@angular/core';
import { Router } from '@angular/router';

const router = inject(Router);

function preloadSettings() {
  router.preload('settings');
}
```

You can call this function when a user hovers over a link or opens a submenu:

```
<a routerLink="/settings"
(mouseover)="preloadSettings()">Settings</a>
```

This technique gives you precise, interaction-based preloading.

For a reactive version using Signals:

```
import { signal, effect } from '@angular/core';
import { Router } from '@angular/router';

const hovered = signal(false);
const router = inject(Router);

effect(() => {
  if (hovered()) {
    router.preload('settings');
  }
});
```

Bind it in your template:

```
<a routerLink="/settings"
(mouseenter)="hovered.set(true)">Settings</a>
```

This kind of UX-driven preloading feels instant to the user—because the code has already arrived by the time they click.

Combining Preloading with Lazy Loading

These techniques aren't exclusive—you can mix and match:

Define most features as lazy-loaded to reduce the initial bundle.

Use `PreloadAllModules` for high-frequency routes.

Use custom strategies for conditional routes.

Use on-demand preloading triggered by user behavior.

Here's a sample route configuration using all of them:

```
const routes: Routes = [
  {
```

```
    path: 'dashboard',
    loadComponent: () =>
import('./dashboard.component').then(m =>
m.DashboardComponent),
    data: { preload: true }
  },
  {
    path: 'reports',
    loadComponent: () =>
import('./reports.component').then(m =>
m.ReportsComponent)
  },
  {
    path: '**',
    redirectTo: ''
  }
];
```

And in your bootstrap configuration:

```
bootstrapApplication(AppComponent, {

  providers: [provideRouter(routes,
withPreloading(SelectivePreloadStrategy))]

});
```

This structure ensures:

dashboard is preloaded after the app boots.

reports is lazy-loaded only when needed.

A fallback redirect handles unknown routes.

Debugging and Monitoring Preloading

To verify that preloading is working:

Open your browser's **Network tab**.

Look for background XHR requests or dynamic *.js chunks being fetched after initial load.

Use Angular DevTools to inspect router configuration and loaded routes.

If you're using custom strategies or manual preloading, it's also helpful to log which routes are preloaded:

```
console.log('Preloading route:', route.path);
```

This will help you fine-tune which features are worth preloading and which should remain lazy.

Preloading isn't just a performance tweak—it's a user experience improvement tool. By fetching lazily loaded routes **before** the user clicks, you reduce delay, eliminate spinners, and make navigation feel seamless.

With Angular 19.2, you can:

Use `PreloadAllModules` for eager background loading.

Create custom strategies to control preload behavior.

Manually preload routes based on UI signals or user behavior.

This gives you complete control over balancing performance and responsiveness—ensuring your app loads quickly, behaves smoothly, and scales effectively.

Chapter 6: Services, Dependency Injection, and HTTP Communication

In Angular, components handle the view layer, but it's services that handle your application logic—data fetching, caching, shared state, and communication with backend APIs. Services in Angular are not just plain TypeScript classes; they're deeply integrated into Angular's **dependency injection (DI)** system, which is a foundational design pattern that promotes loose coupling, testability, and maintainability.

Creating and Injecting Services

In Angular, services are used to encapsulate business logic, data access, and shared functionality that doesn't belong in your components. Components are responsible for presenting data and handling user interaction; services take care of logic that persists beyond a single view—like managing authentication, fetching data, or coordinating actions between multiple components.

At the core of Angular's service architecture is **dependency injection (DI)**. This mechanism allows Angular to create and supply the dependencies your components and services need, without you having to construct them manually.

What is a Service in Angular?

A service in Angular is any class that provides functionality and is decorated with the `@Injectable()` decorator. This decorator tells Angular that it can inject this service into other classes through the DI system.

Here's a basic example:

```
import { Injectable } from '@angular/core';

@Injectable({ providedIn: 'root' })
export class LoggerService {
  log(message: string) {
    console.log(`[LOG]: ${message}`);
  }
```

```
}
```

The `@Injectable({ providedIn: 'root' })` syntax is a **tree-shakable provider**—it automatically registers this service in Angular's root injector and ensures a single shared instance across the application.

You can now inject this service into any component or service without needing to register it in a module or providers array.

Injecting a Service into a Component

Let's say you want to display a list of log messages inside a component. You start by injecting the service into the component's constructor.

```
import { Component } from '@angular/core';
import { LoggerService } from './logger.service';

@Component({
  selector: 'app-log-panel',
  standalone: true,
  template: `
    <h3>Logger Panel</h3>
    <button (click)="writeLog()">Write Log</button>
  `
})
export class LogPanelComponent {
  constructor(private logger: LoggerService) {}

  writeLog() {
    this.logger.log('Log button clicked');
  }
}
```

Angular sees that `LoggerService` is requested in the constructor, looks it up in the DI tree (starting from this component), and provides the instance defined in `providedIn: 'root'`.

You don't need to create the service manually or call `new LoggerService()`—Angular handles lifecycle and instantiation, and ensures there's only one instance unless you explicitly scope it otherwise.

Injecting Services into Other Services

You're not limited to injecting services into components. Services can depend on other services, too. Angular builds a graph of dependencies and resolves them recursively.

Let's build a UserService that logs when a user is fetched.

```
@Injectable({ providedIn: 'root' })
export class UserService {
  constructor(private logger: LoggerService) {}

  getUserById(id: number): string {
    this.logger.log(`Fetching user with ID:
${id}`);
    return `User-${id}`;
  }
}
```

And in your component:

```
export class UserComponent {
  constructor(private userService: UserService) {}

  ngOnInit() {
    const user = this.userService.getUserById(1);
    console.log(user);
  }
}
```

Angular handles the injection chain:

UserComponent gets UserService

UserService gets LoggerService

Both are singletons by default (since both use providedIn: 'root')

This allows you to compose complex services from simple, testable building blocks.

Using inject() for Function-Based Injection

In Angular 14+, and used extensively in Angular 15–19+, Angular introduced the inject() function, which allows you to access services **outside of a**

constructor. This is especially useful in **standalone functions**, **interceptors**, and **functional services**.

Example:

```
import { inject } from '@angular/core';

@Injectable({ providedIn: 'root' })
export class TokenService {
  private storage = inject(StorageService);

  getToken(): string | null {
    return this.storage.get('auth_token');
  }
}
```

This lets you use injected dependencies without needing to declare them in the constructor, which simplifies service code—especially for utility services with multiple internal dependencies.

Injecting Services in Standalone Components

In Angular 19.2, where standalone components are now the recommended default, injection works the same way. Here's a real-world component using a service:

```
import { Component } from '@angular/core';
import { CounterService } from './counter.service';

@Component({
  selector: 'app-counter',
  standalone: true,
  template: `
    <p>Count: {{ counter.value }}</p>
    <button
(click)="counter.increment()">+1</button>
  `,
  providers: [CounterService] // scoped to this
component
})
export class CounterComponent {
  constructor(public counter: CounterService) {}
}
```

By including the service in the `providers` array of the component, you scope the service instance to that component alone. Every instance of `CounterComponent` gets its own `CounterService`.

This is excellent for encapsulating state in widgets, nested UIs, or isolated forms.

Testing Injected Services

Angular's DI system also makes services very easy to test. You can provide mock versions of services using Angular's testing utilities.

Example:

```
describe('UserService', () => {
  let service: UserService;
  let logger: jasmine.SpyObj<LoggerService>;

  beforeEach(() => {
    logger = jasmine.createSpyObj('LoggerService',
['log']);
    TestBed.configureTestingModule({
      providers: [
        UserService,
        { provide: LoggerService, useValue: logger
}
      ]
    });

    service = TestBed.inject(UserService);
  });

  it('should call logger when fetching user', () =>
{
    service.getUserById(1);

expect(logger.log).toHaveBeenCalledWith('Fetching
user with ID: 1');
  });
});
```

Mocking injected services lets you isolate behavior and verify dependencies are used correctly, without triggering external side effects.

Common Pitfalls to Avoid

Creating services with `new` manually – Avoid doing this. It bypasses Angular's DI system and defeats testability and singleton behavior.

Forgetting `@Injectable()` – Without the decorator, Angular won't know how to inject the service, and you'll see an error like "No provider for..."

Conflicting provider scopes – Defining a service in both a component and module can lead to different instances being created in unexpected places.

Injecting services without using DI tokens – When providing non-class values (like config objects), use `InjectionToken` to ensure type safety and injection clarity.

Real-World Use Case

In a real app, services are where the bulk of your logic lives:

A `UserService` fetches and caches user profiles.

An `AuthService` manages login, token storage, and session expiration.

A `CartService` tracks shopping cart items across pages.

A `LoggerService` records actions and sends them to a backend log aggregator.

By isolating this logic, your components stay lightweight, focused, and easier to reason about. Services also make your codebase easier to test, mock, refactor, and reuse across multiple views.

Creating and injecting services is one of the fundamental skills in Angular. It's not just about moving logic out of components—it's about creating clean, composable, and decoupled application architecture. With Angular's dependency injection model, you get powerful scoping, testability, and reusability built right in.

Scoped Providers and Hierarchical DI

Angular's **hierarchical dependency injection** model is one of its most powerful architectural features. It enables you to control *where* and *how long* services live in your application. Instead of being limited to one global instance of a service, Angular allows you to **scope** services at different levels in the component tree or route structure. This gives you precise control over service lifecycles, memory usage, and state isolation.

Understanding Angular's Injector Tree

Angular maintains a **hierarchy of injectors**, starting from the root injector. When you inject a service into a class, Angular looks for that service starting from the closest injector:

The component's own injector.

The parent component's injector.

The root injector.

This lookup continues up the tree until Angular either finds a match or throws an error if no provider is found.

So when you declare a service with `providedIn: 'root'`, you're registering it with the application-wide root injector. That means **a single instance** is shared across the entire application.

However, you can override this by providing a service in a **component** or **route**. Angular will then create **a new instance scoped to that injector**, isolated from the rest of the app.

Component-Scoped Services

Let's say you're building a `<quiz-section>` component, and each instance of this component should have its own score tracker. You don't want to share state between multiple quizzes shown on the same page.

First, define the service:

```
import { Injectable } from '@angular/core';

@Injectable()
export class ScoreService {
  private _score = 0;

  increment() {
    this._score++;
```

```
    }

    get score(): number {
      return this._score;
    }
}
```

Now provide it at the component level:

```
import { Component } from '@angular/core';
import { ScoreService } from './score.service';

@Component({
  selector: 'app-quiz-section',
  standalone: true,
  template: `
    <h3>Score: {{ scoreService.score }}</h3>
    <button
(click)="scoreService.increment()">Answer
Correct</button>
  `,
  providers: [ScoreService]
})
export class QuizSectionComponent {
  constructor(public scoreService: ScoreService) {}
}
```

Every time this component is created, Angular creates a **new instance** of ScoreService—so each quiz section tracks its own score independently.

This is especially useful when:

The state is localized and shouldn't leak.

You want easy teardown of service instances when the component is destroyed.

You want testable, reusable components with self-contained logic.

Route-Scoped Services

With Angular 15 and beyond, including 19.2, Angular allows you to define services at the **route level**, making it easier to scope logic per feature or view.

Here's a `UserService` that should only be available while viewing a particular user route.

First, define the service:

```
@Injectable()

export class UserService {

  getUserInfo(id: string) {

    return { name: `User ${id}`, id };

  }

}
```

Then provide it in the route definition:

```
{

  path: 'profile/:id',

  component: ProfileComponent,

  providers: [UserService]

}
```

Now inside `ProfileComponent`, you can safely inject `UserService`:

```
@Component({
  selector: 'app-profile',
  standalone: true,
  template: `<p>{{ user?.name }}</p>`
})
export class ProfileComponent implements OnInit {
  user: any;

  constructor(
    private route: ActivatedRoute,
    private userService: UserService
  ) {}
```

```
  ngOnInit() {
    const id =
this.route.snapshot.paramMap.get('id')!;
    this.user = this.userService.getUserInfo(id);
  }
}
```

Each time the user navigates to a different `/profile/:id`, Angular instantiates a **new route-scoped `UserService`**, which gets destroyed when the route is left. This keeps feature-specific state clean and encapsulated.

Use cases:

Wizards with multi-step logic.

Feature modules with internal services.

Stateful modals or dashboards.

Analytics tracking tied to views.

How Angular Resolves Conflicts

When multiple providers exist for the same service, Angular chooses the **nearest provider** in the injector hierarchy.

Example:

You register `SettingsService` in the root.

You provide a different version of `SettingsService` in `AccountComponent`.

Any child of `AccountComponent` that requests `SettingsService` will receive the component-scoped version. Siblings or unrelated components continue to receive the root instance.

This makes it easy to:

Override services for specific features.

Mock services in certain components (e.g., testing).

Swap implementations conditionally.

Sharing State Across Components: When to Avoid Local Scope

While component-scoped services are powerful, use them when **isolation** is your goal. If you want to **share state** between sibling components or across pages, register your service at a higher level:

Use `providedIn: 'root'` for app-wide singletons.

Register at a feature module level if scoping to that module.

Register at a layout or shared container component if scoping to a page group.

For example, a `CartService` that tracks a user's shopping cart should be shared. It should not be scoped to each product component or route, otherwise you'll lose cart contents on navigation.

Best Practices for Scoped DI

Scope services intentionally. Don't default to root if the logic is highly localized.

Prefer route providers for short-lived feature-specific services.

Use component providers for embedded or interactive UI widgets.

Avoid using both `providedIn: 'root'` and local `providers: [...]`—this can cause confusion.

Consider signals, observables, or stores within the service if state needs to be reactive.

Example: A Chat Widget With Scoped State

Suppose you have a reusable chat widget that appears in various parts of the app, and you want each one to have its own message history.

```
@Injectable()
export class ChatService {
  private messages: string[] = [];

  send(message: string) {
    this.messages.push(message);
  }

  getHistory(): string[] {
    return this.messages;
```

```
    }
}
```

Provided in the component:

```
@Component({
  selector: 'app-chat-widget',
  standalone: true,
  template: `
    <input [(ngModel)]="msg" />
    <button (click)="send()">Send</button>
    <div *ngFor="let m of history">{{ m }}</div>
  `,
  providers: [ChatService]
})
export class ChatWidgetComponent {
  msg = '';

  constructor(public chat: ChatService) {}

  send() {
    this.chat.send(this.msg);
    this.msg = '';
  }

  get history() {
    return this.chat.getHistory();
  }
}
```

Every widget manages its own message state, without conflicts or shared memory.

Angular's hierarchical dependency injection system allows you to control the lifecycle, scope, and visibility of services precisely. By scoping services at the component or route level, you gain memory efficiency, state encapsulation, and better architectural separation. Understanding how Angular resolves dependencies enables you to build scalable applications where logic is cleanly isolated and reused intelligently.

HTTP Client for RESTful APIs

Angular's `HttpClient` is your gateway to working with backend APIs in a structured, reactive, and type-safe way. It's built into the Angular framework via the `@angular/common/http` package and is fully integrated with Angular's dependency injection system and the `Observable` pattern provided by RxJS.

The goal of this section is to give you a clear understanding of how `HttpClient` works in practice—from basic GET requests to full CRUD operations. You'll also see how to handle query parameters, headers, typed responses, and how to structure your code for clarity and maintainability.

Registering the HttpClient Module

To use `HttpClient`, you need to register it in your application during bootstrap. Angular 16+ makes this easy with `provideHttpClient()`:

```
import { provideHttpClient } from
'@angular/common/http';


bootstrapApplication(AppComponent, {

  providers: [provideHttpClient()]

});
```

Once registered, you can inject `HttpClient` anywhere it's needed—typically inside a service class.

Performing Basic GET Requests

To perform HTTP requests, inject `HttpClient` into your service and use its methods such as `.get()`, `.post()`, `.put()`, and `.delete()`.

Here's a service that fetches a list of users from a backend:

```
import { Injectable } from '@angular/core';
import { HttpClient } from '@angular/common/http';
import { Observable } from 'rxjs';
```

```
export interface User {
  id: number;
  name: string;
  email: string;
}

@Injectable({ providedIn: 'root' })
export class UserService {
  private readonly apiUrl = '/api/users';

  constructor(private http: HttpClient) {}

  getUsers(): Observable<User[]> {
    return this.http.get<User[]>(this.apiUrl);
  }
}
```

This method returns an `Observable` of `User[]`. Angular's `HttpClient` automatically parses the JSON response and casts it to the type you specify.

In your component:

```
export class UserListComponent implements OnInit {
  users: User[] = [];

  constructor(private userService: UserService) {}

  ngOnInit() {
    this.userService.getUsers().subscribe(data => {
      this.users = data;
    });
  }
}
```

The `subscribe()` call starts the HTTP request and delivers the response when ready. Since `HttpClient` uses observables, you can also apply operators like `map()`, `filter()`, `catchError()` for transformation and error handling.

GET with Query Parameters

Let's say your API supports filtering users via a search term. Angular's `HttpParams` class helps you construct query strings cleanly.

```
import { HttpParams } from '@angular/common/http';

searchUsers(query: string): Observable<User[]> {
  const params = new HttpParams().set('q', query);
  return this.http.get<User[]>(this.apiUrl, {
params });
}
```

This will generate a request like:

GET /api/users?q=searchTerm

You can chain multiple `.set()` calls or use `.append()` to handle multiple values for the same key.

Making POST Requests

To create a new resource, use `.post()`:

```
createUser(user: Partial<User>): Observable<User> {

  return this.http.post<User>(this.apiUrl, user);

}
```

In this example, `Partial<User>` allows sending only name and email without the ID (which might be generated by the server). Angular serializes the object to JSON automatically and sets `Content-Type: application/json`.

You can provide headers manually if needed:

```
const headers = new
HttpHeaders().set('Authorization', 'Bearer token');

this.http.post<User>(this.apiUrl, user, { headers
});
```

Updating and Deleting Data

Updating a user:

```
updateUser(id: number, user: Partial<User>):
Observable<User> {
  return
this.http.put<User>(`${this.apiUrl}/${id}`, user);
```

```
}
```

Deleting a user:

```
deleteUser(id: number): Observable<void> {
  return
this.http.delete<void>(`${this.apiUrl}/${id}`);
}
```

The use of string interpolation (`${ }`) ensures the right endpoint URL.

Handling Errors Gracefully

Always handle errors when working with HTTP requests. Use `catchError()` to intercept and respond to errors.

```
import { catchError } from 'rxjs/operators';
import { throwError } from 'rxjs';

getUsers(): Observable<User[]> {
  return this.http.get<User[]>(this.apiUrl).pipe(
    catchError(error => {
      console.error('Failed to load users', error);
      return throwError(() => new Error('Something
went wrong'));
    })
  );
}
```

You can then show a user-friendly error message or trigger fallback logic.

Typing Responses for Safety

Strong typing is essential for reliability. Always define interfaces for your response models and use them in your HTTP methods.

Avoid using `any` unless absolutely necessary. TypeScript can't help you if you discard type safety.

Example interface:

```
export interface ApiResponse<T> {
  data: T;
  status: string;
```

```
}
```

Typed usage:

```
getUsers(): Observable<ApiResponse<User[]>> {

  return
this.http.get<ApiResponse<User[]>>(this.apiUrl);

}
```

You'll now get proper type inference when accessing `response.data` or `response.status`.

Injecting HttpClient into Services with Signals

In Angular 19.2, it's common to use Signals to manage state within services. Here's how to combine Signals and `HttpClient`:

```
import { signal } from '@angular/core';

@Injectable({ providedIn: 'root' })
export class PostService {
  private posts = signal<Post[]>([]);
  readonly posts$ = this.posts.asReadonly();

  constructor(private http: HttpClient) {}

  loadPosts() {
this.http.get<Post[]>('/api/posts').subscribe(posts
=> {
      this.posts.set(posts);
    });
  }
}
```

This setup lets your components use `posts$()` as a reactive signal-bound state.

Real-World Example: Paginated and Filtered Requests

You might have an API like:

```
GET /api/products?page=2&pageSize=10&category=books
```

Service method:

```
getProducts(page: number, pageSize: number,
category?: string): Observable<Product[]> {
  let params = new HttpParams()
    .set('page', page)
    .set('pageSize', pageSize);

  if (category) {
    params = params.set('category', category);
  }

  return this.http.get<Product[]>('/api/products',
{ params });
}
```

This is clean, testable, and reusable—and maps perfectly to REST APIs with advanced filtering needs.

Summary

Angular's `HttpClient` is a powerful abstraction over browser `fetch()` or `XMLHttpRequest`, giving you:

Fully typed responses

RxJS-based reactive control

Automatic JSON handling

Declarative API for headers, query params, and error management

By structuring your HTTP calls inside services, handling errors consistently, and leveraging Angular's DI and signal system, you ensure that your data layer is robust, predictable, and easy to maintain.

Interceptors and Error Handling Strategies

When working with HTTP in Angular applications, consistency is everything. You don't want to repeat the same code across dozens of services for things like attaching authentication tokens, handling timeouts, transforming responses, or dealing with errors. This is where **HTTP interceptors** come in.

Interceptors allow you to **hook into the request/response lifecycle** and apply logic globally to all outgoing requests and incoming responses.

An interceptor is simply a function that Angular calls for every HTTP request. It allows you to modify the request or response—or handle errors centrally. Interceptors are part of Angular's `HttpClient` module and work seamlessly with all observable-based HTTP methods.

Interceptors are powerful for:

Attaching auth tokens or API keys

Logging requests and responses

Handling global errors

Transforming response data formats

Retrying failed requests automatically

Blocking or redirecting based on HTTP status

Creating a Simple Auth Token Interceptor

Here's a service that holds an access token:

```
@Injectable({ providedIn: 'root' })
export class AuthService {
  private token: string | null = 'mock-token-123';

  getToken(): string | null {
    return this.token;
  }
}
```

Now let's create a functional interceptor that attaches this token to all HTTP requests:

```
import { HttpInterceptorFn } from
'@angular/common/http';
import { inject } from '@angular/core';
import { AuthService } from './auth.service';
```

```
export const authInterceptor: HttpInterceptorFn =
(req, next) => {
  const auth = inject(AuthService);
  const token = auth.getToken();

  const authReq = token
    ? req.clone({ setHeaders: { Authorization:
`Bearer ${token}` } })
    : req;

  return next(authReq);
};
```

You clone the original request and attach the `Authorization` header if a token is present. This cloned request is then passed along the chain using `next()`.

To activate the interceptor, register it with `provideHttpClient()`:

```
import { provideHttpClient, withInterceptors } from
'@angular/common/http';

bootstrapApplication(AppComponent, {
  providers: [

provideHttpClient(withInterceptors([authInterceptor
]))
  ]
});
```

All requests from this point forward automatically include the token—without any changes in individual services.

Building a Global Error Handler Interceptor

Handling errors consistently improves UX and makes debugging easier. Here's a functional interceptor that catches HTTP errors and handles them centrally:

```
import { HttpInterceptorFn } from
'@angular/common/http';
import { catchError, throwError } from 'rxjs';
import { inject } from '@angular/core';
import { Router } from '@angular/router';
```

```
export const errorInterceptor: HttpInterceptorFn =
(req, next) => {
  const router = inject(Router);

  return next(req).pipe(
    catchError(error => {
      if (error.status === 401) {
        router.navigate(['/login']);
      }

      if (error.status >= 500) {
        console.error('Server error occurred',
error);
      }

      return throwError(() => error);
    })
  );
};
```

This interceptor:

Redirects the user to the login page on `401 Unauthorized`

Logs any server-side error (`500+`)

Allows individual components or services to further react to the error, since it's still being thrown

You can chain it alongside the auth interceptor:

```
provideHttpClient(withInterceptors([authInterceptor
, errorInterceptor]))
```

Angular will apply these interceptors **in the order they are declared** for requests, and in **reverse order** for responses.

Retrying Failed Requests

Sometimes, requests fail temporarily due to network hiccups. Angular gives you the ability to retry failed requests using RxJS's `retry` or `retryWhen`.

Here's how to retry up to 3 times:

```
import { retry } from 'rxjs';

export const retryInterceptor: HttpInterceptorFn =
(req, next) => {
  return next(req).pipe(retry(3));
};
```

To combine all three:

```
provideHttpClient(

  withInterceptors([

    authInterceptor,

    retryInterceptor,

    errorInterceptor

  ])

)
```

This will:

Add the auth token

Retry failed requests up to 3 times

Redirect or log errors depending on status

Each interceptor does one job—and together, they cover all concerns.

Logging Requests and Responses

If you want to log all outgoing requests and responses for debugging or metrics:

```
export const loggingInterceptor: HttpInterceptorFn
= (req, next) => {
  console.log('Outgoing request:', req);

  return next(req).pipe(
    tap(response => {
      console.log('Incoming response:', response);
```

```
    })
  );
};
```

You can enhance this by logging durations, request sizes, or tagging routes for analytics.

Handling Different Error Types

You can tailor your error handling based on whether the error came from the client side (e.g., no internet connection) or server side (e.g., bad API response):

```
catchError(error => {
  if (error.error instanceof ErrorEvent) {
    console.error('Client-side error:',
error.error.message);
  } else {
    console.error(`Server returned
${error.status}:`, error.message);
  }

  return throwError(() => error);
})
```

This gives you more clarity in error logs and helps separate network failures from server failures.

Best Practices for Interceptors and Error Handling

Keep interceptors **focused**—each should do one thing well.

Use **functional interceptors** (`HttpInterceptorFn`) instead of class-based ones unless you need lifecycle hooks.

Don't silently swallow errors. Always log or propagate them.

Use route guards for full-page redirects; use interceptors for lightweight logic.

Centralize retry logic—don't spread retries across different services.

Never hardcode URLs or tokens in interceptors—use injected services.

Real-World Use Case: Secured App with Centralized Error Handling

You're building an admin dashboard with:

Protected routes (`/admin`, `/settings`)

Token-based auth

Backend prone to occasional server hiccups

Use this stack:

`authInterceptor`: adds the bearer token

`retryInterceptor`: retries up to 2 times

`errorInterceptor`: logs and redirects on 401

This ensures:

Consistent API authentication

Tolerance for network instability

Graceful user redirection if sessions expire

Your app feels faster, safer, and more predictable—and you've removed all boilerplate from your components and services.

Interceptors give you a way to enforce global rules for how HTTP works in your Angular app. Whether it's injecting headers, handling errors, retrying failed requests, or logging for observability—interceptors help keep your code centralized, maintainable, and consistent.

By applying interceptors strategically and pairing them with Angular's `HttpClient`, you gain full control over how your application communicates with external services—ensuring that your app behaves reliably and provides meaningful feedback to users when things go wrong.

Chapter 7: Building for Scale and Maintainability

As Angular projects grow, so does the complexity of managing features, organizing code, sharing logic, and enforcing consistency. What starts as a few components and services can quickly become hundreds of files spanning multiple teams and domains. Without structure, maintainability suffers.

This chapter focuses on how to **architect Angular projects for long-term scalability**. You'll learn about Angular's **modular design principles**, how to separate concerns with **feature, shared, and core modules**, how to organize your file structure consistently, and how to **configure environment-specific settings** using Angular's built-in tooling. Whether you're working solo or leading a team, the practices here will help you build apps that are organized, testable, and easy to onboard into.

Modular Architecture in Angular

As your Angular application grows from a few components into a large-scale system with multiple teams and features, **modular architecture** becomes essential. It's the strategy that allows you to build isolated, reusable, and maintainable features—each with its own components, services, routing, and even styles. Whether you are using traditional `NgModule`-based architecture or standalone components introduced in Angular 15+, modular design principles remain foundational for organizing scalable Angular codebases.

In Angular, a module is a boundary that encapsulates a **specific set of functionality**—it could represent a feature (like Orders), a concern (like Authentication), or a shared utility (like a button library).

Modular architecture allows you to:

Isolate features and domain logic.

Enable lazy loading to optimize performance.

Improve testability by reducing dependencies.

Promote team-based development with clearly defined ownership.

You don't have to rely exclusively on `NgModule` for modularity. Angular 19.2 supports full application architecture with **standalone components**. The key takeaway is this: **modular design is about logical separation, not syntax**.

Modular Thinking: Feature-First, Not Type-First

A common mistake in early Angular projects is organizing code by type:

`/components`

`/services`

`/models`

This doesn't scale well. As features grow, you lose context, and files get scattered. Modular Angular architecture favors **feature-based structure**, grouping everything by the functional area it supports.

For example, a `Users` feature might have:

`/src/app/users/`

    ├── `users.routes.ts`

    ├── `user-list.component.ts`

    ├── `user-form.component.ts`

    ├── `user.service.ts`

    ├── `user.model.ts`

Each folder owns its logic. You no longer have to jump between directories to understand how a feature works or to onboard a new developer into a domain area.

Module Composition Using Standalone Components

With standalone components, Angular allows you to build self-contained features without writing `NgModules`. Here's a practical example:

```
// user-list.component.ts
@Component({
  selector: 'app-user-list',
  standalone: true,
```

```
  imports: [CommonModule],
  template: `
    <div *ngFor="let user of users">{{ user.name
}}</div>
  `
})
export class UserListComponent {
  users = [{ name: 'Alice' }, { name: 'Bob' }];
}
```

Standalone components can be declared, routed, and lazily loaded without being bundled inside an NgModule:

```
export const USER_ROUTES: Routes = [
  {
    path: '',
    component: UserListComponent
  }
];
```

Lazy load it:

```
{

  path: 'users',

  loadChildren: () =>
import('./users/users.routes').then(m =>
m.USER_ROUTES)
}
```

This setup reduces boilerplate and promotes smaller, focused units of composition. Each component or route is part of the app's modular structure, regardless of whether it uses a module or not.

When to Use NgModule

While standalone components are the future-facing approach, NgModule still has its place in some scenarios:

If you're maintaining a legacy app.

When using libraries that require NgModule compatibility.

When grouping a collection of third-party modules and declarations (e.g., a shared UI module).

Here's a traditional **UsersModule**:

```
@NgModule({

  declarations: [UserListComponent,
UserFormComponent],

  imports: [CommonModule, FormsModule],

  exports: [UserListComponent]

})

export class UsersModule {}
```

This module bundles related components and services. In a hybrid app, you can mix both traditional modules and standalone components as needed.

Designing Modular Boundaries for Teams

If multiple teams are working on the same Angular project, you can divide your app into **well-defined feature modules**, where each team owns a slice of the application.

For example:

```
/src/app/
    ├── users/          ← Owned by Team A
    ├── orders/         ← Owned by Team B
    ├── reports/        ← Owned by Team C
    └── shared/         ← Common components, pipes
```

Each team can:

Maintain their own routing structure (users.routes.ts, orders.routes.ts)

Define scoped services like UserService, OrderService

Use route-level providers to scope dependency instances

This reduces merge conflicts, eases onboarding, and simplifies ownership reviews during PRs.

How Lazy Loading Works with Modular Features

Lazy loading is a critical part of Angular's modular story. It allows you to split your application into **chunks** that are loaded only when needed.

Let's say you have a `ReportsComponent` defined as standalone:

```
export const REPORTS_ROUTES: Routes = [

  {

    path: '',

    loadComponent: () =>

      import('./reports.component').then(m =>
m.ReportsComponent)

  }

];
```

You can then lazy load it in the main route configuration:

```
{

  path: 'reports',

  loadChildren: () =>
import('./reports/reports.routes').then(m =>
m.REPORTS_ROUTES)

}
```

With this in place:

The `ReportsComponent` and its dependencies won't be loaded until the user visits `/reports`.

You save bandwidth and reduce the initial load time of the app.

Each feature can evolve independently, with its own scoped logic and routing.

Scalability Through Isolation

Modular architecture isn't just about organizing files. It's about **isolation**. Each module or feature directory should:

Own its dependencies.

Avoid global state when possible.

Export only what other features need.

Avoid direct imports from other feature modules.

If a service, component, or pipe is needed in multiple places, move it to `shared/`. If it's specific to one area, keep it inside that feature module.

This encourages reuse without tight coupling, allowing large teams to work in parallel without stepping on each other's toes.

Modular architecture is what makes Angular sustainable in large applications. By grouping your logic into isolated, meaningful units—whether with `NgModules` or standalone components—you keep your application easier to understand, easier to test, and easier to extend.

Angular gives you the flexibility to apply modular thinking across components, routes, services, and directories. The key is consistency: define clear boundaries, isolate state where possible, and build with growth in mind.

Feature Modules, Shared Modules, and Core Modules

In any Angular application that's expected to grow, managing complexity isn't just about writing good components—it's about organizing those components, services, and utilities into **clear, predictable boundaries**. Angular supports this with the concept of modularization, and in practice, three types of modules help you maintain a clean architecture: **feature modules**, **shared modules**, and **core modules**.

Each serves a distinct purpose. Knowing when and how to use each one prevents tight coupling, improves testability, enables lazy loading, and keeps your development experience smooth as your app scales.

Feature Modules: Functional Isolation

A **feature module** encapsulates everything related to a specific business function or section of your app. Think of it as a vertical slice—components, services, models, and routes that all relate to one bounded context.

Suppose you have a users section in your app. You would organize it like this:

/src/app/users/

    ├── **user-list.component.ts**

    ├── **user-detail.component.ts**

    ├── **user-form.component.ts**

    ├── **user.service.ts**

    ├── **user.model.ts**

    └── **users.routes.ts**

You can use either `NgModule` or the standalone component approach introduced in Angular 15+. Both support lazy loading and route scoping.

Using standalone routing (recommended for Angular 15+):

```
export const USERS_ROUTES: Routes = [
  {
    path: '',
    component: UserListComponent
  },
  {
    path: ':id',
    component: UserDetailComponent
  }
];
```

Lazy load this route set in your root route config:

```
{
```

```
  path: 'users',
  loadChildren: () =>
import('./users/users.routes').then(m =>
m.USERS_ROUTES)
}
```

Each feature should manage its own:
Routing

Services

State

UI components

Avoid importing services or components directly from another feature. If reuse is needed, elevate them to the **shared** module instead.

Shared Module: Reusable UI Building Blocks

The **shared module** contains reusable pieces that **do not depend on any business logic**. These are usually stateless, pure, and broadly applicable across features. Examples include:

Common UI components like buttons, modals, and tables

Pipes like `capitalize`, `truncate`, or `currencyFormat`

Directives like `autoFocus`, `highlight`, or `formControlError`

Utility interfaces or lightweight services with no side effects

Folder structure:

/src/app/shared/

    ├── **components/**

    │   └── **button.component.ts**

    ├── **directives/**

    │   └── **autofocus.directive.ts**

    ├── **pipes/**

```
|     └── capitalize.pipe.ts
├── shared.module.ts (optional)
└── index.ts
```

With standalone components, you often don't need `shared.module.ts`. Instead, define a barrel file (`index.ts`) and import/export everything you want to expose:

```
export * from './components/button.component';

export * from './directives/autofocus.directive';

export * from './pipes/capitalize.pipe';
```

Now you can import shared features like this:

```
import { ButtonComponent } from '@app/shared';
```

This improves discoverability and ensures that all commonly used UI utilities are maintained in a single location.

Do not place services with side effects, API logic, or feature logic in the shared module. That's the responsibility of the **core** or **feature** modules.

Core Module: Application Infrastructure and Singletons

The **core module** contains the **singleton services and app-wide logic** that should exist only once and be available throughout the entire application. This includes:

Authentication and authorization services

Global interceptors

App-wide configuration and constants

Logging and analytics

Guards and route resolvers

Typical folder layout:

/src/app/core/

```
├── services/
│     ├── auth.service.ts
│     ├── logger.service.ts
│     └── config.service.ts
├── guards/
├── interceptors/
├── core.module.ts (optional)
└── index.ts
```

You don't need to import `CoreModule` into components. Instead, you register services using Angular's modern provider API:

```
bootstrapApplication(AppComponent, {

  providers: [

provideHttpClient(withInterceptors([authInterceptor
, errorInterceptor])),

    AuthService,

    ConfigService,

    LoggerService

  ]
});
```

If you are still using `CoreModule`, ensure that it is imported only once in your app—preferably in the root module (if your app uses one). Never import the core module into feature or shared modules, or you may end up with duplicate singleton instances.

Singleton Rule: Anything meant to exist only once in the app should go in the core module.

Distinguishing the Roles of Each Module

Let's break this down into practical terms with a feature example: **User Management**.

Where should each of the following live?

Item	Correct Module	Why
`UserListComponent`	Feature (Users)	Specific to the user feature
`UserService`	Feature (Users)	Tied to user domain
`AuthService`	Core	Used across the entire app
`ButtonComponent`	Shared	Generic UI control
`CapitalizePipe`	Shared	Reusable transformation
`AuthGuard`	Core	Shared routing logic

This boundary discipline ensures that responsibilities don't blur. Each module becomes easy to reason about and change independently.

How They Work Together

To build your application properly:

Lazy load **feature modules** so they aren't bundled in the main bundle.

Import **shared module exports** in each feature or route that needs them.

Register global services in the **core module** or root provider configuration.

If you're using standalone components, you don't need the boilerplate of NgModule. But the **logical modular boundaries** are still just as important. The folder structure and separation of concerns remain.

Real-World Scenario: Scaling a Multi-Team Angular App

Let's say your Angular app supports users, analytics, billing, and support. Each of these is a **feature module**, owned by a different team. They use shared components like tables and charts, and all share app-wide services for authentication, logging, and environment configuration.

Your structure would look like this:

```
/src/app/
    ├── users/
    ├── analytics/
    ├── billing/
    ├── support/
    ├── shared/
    ├── core/
    └── app.routes.ts
```

Each team works in their feature directory. They all consume reusable UI from `shared/`, and services from `core/`. This keeps team boundaries clean and app startup performance optimized through lazy loading.

Modular design in Angular isn't optional in real-world applications—it's the foundation of maintainability and clarity. By clearly separating your app into **feature modules**, **shared utilities**, and **core infrastructure**, you build a structure that supports growth without collapsing under its own weight.

File Structure and Naming Conventions

One of the most overlooked but critical aspects of building a maintainable Angular application is how you organize your files and name them. When a project is small, poor structure may go unnoticed. But as soon as your team grows or you start adding dozens of features, poorly named or scattered files make collaboration and debugging unnecessarily hard.

A clean, predictable file structure doesn't just help with readability—it dramatically improves navigation, refactoring, testing, and onboarding. This section outlines a set of proven practices that will help you organize your

Angular app for clarity and long-term stability, regardless of whether you're using standalone components or traditional modules.

Feature-First Structure Over Type-First

In Angular's early days, it was common to organize projects by file type:

`/components`

`/services`

`/models`

But this quickly breaks down in large apps because related pieces of functionality are spread across directories. You end up jumping between folders just to understand how a single feature works.

The modern Angular practice is **feature-first**: group all the files related to a single feature—components, services, pipes, routes, models—into a single folder. This aligns with how humans think about software: by feature, not by file extension.

Example of a well-structured feature directory:

`/src/app/users/`

```
├── user-list.component.ts
├── user-form.component.ts
├── user-detail.component.ts
├── user.service.ts
├── user.model.ts
├── users.routes.ts
└── index.ts
```

Everything related to the **Users** feature is self-contained, making it easy to work on or test without worrying about the rest of the codebase.

Naming Files for Predictability

Angular uses file suffixes to differentiate file types, and following these conventions helps both your team and tooling (like Angular Language Service, Jest, or ESLint) understand what each file contains.

Here are the naming patterns that should be followed consistently across your app:

Components: `user-list.component.ts`

Templates: `user-list.component.html`

Styles: `user-list.component.scss`

Services: `user.service.ts`

Interfaces/Types: `user.model.ts`

Routes: `users.routes.ts`

Pipes: `capitalize.pipe.ts`

Directives: `auto-focus.directive.ts`

Unit Tests: `user-list.component.spec.ts`

Each file name is in **kebab-case**, which aligns with Angular CLI and general community standards. Kebab case avoids casing issues on case-insensitive filesystems and is easier to scan visually.

If you are using a component with inline template and style, still maintain the file name ending with `.component.ts` for clarity:

```
@Component({

  selector: 'app-user-list',

  template: `<div>User List</div>`,

  standalone: true

})

export class UserListComponent {}
```

You don't need `.html` or `.scss` files in that case, but your naming should stay consistent.

Folder Naming

Use lowercase kebab-case for folders, even for features:

/src/app/user-profile/

/src/app/order-history/

/src/app/admin-panel/

This avoids inconsistencies, especially in cross-platform projects, and keeps imports consistent in format:

```
import { UserListComponent } from './user-
profile/user-list.component';
```

For sub-features, nesting is fine but should be shallow. Don't go beyond 2–3 levels deep. Deep nesting makes navigation harder, especially in IDEs.

Barrel Files for Re-Exports

A **barrel file** is an `index.ts` used to re-export everything a module or folder should expose. This simplifies import paths and improves discoverability.

Instead of this:

```
import { UserService } from
'../../users/user.service';
import { UserListComponent } from
'../../users/user-list.component';
```

You can have:

```
import { UserService, UserListComponent } from
'@app/users';
```

This requires an `index.ts` file like:

```
export * from './user.service';

export * from './user-list.component';
```

```
export * from './user-form.component';
```

And a path alias in `tsconfig.json`:

```
"paths": {

  "@app/*": ["src/app/*"]

}
```

Always use `index.ts` to define what is public. Don't blindly re-export everything. Only export what's meant for external consumption to maintain proper encapsulation.

Organizing Standalone Components

If you're using standalone components, treat them as self-contained units. Keep all files related to the component in the same folder.

/src/app/users/user-list/

    ├── **user-list.component.ts**

    ├── **user-list.component.html**

    ├── **user-list.component.scss**

    └── **user-list.component.spec.ts**

This is particularly helpful when components are shared across multiple features. You can even collocate the test and mock data within the same folder for easier maintenance.

When components are part of a larger feature, it's also acceptable to group them flat under the feature directory if they're tightly coupled:

/src/app/orders/

    ├── **order-list.component.ts**

    ├── **order-form.component.ts**

    ├── **order-detail.component.ts**

Choose the pattern that minimizes mental friction and keeps context together.

Routing Files and Route Modules

Always name your route files using the `*.routes.ts` pattern. This makes route entry points easy to find and standardizes lazy-loading across the app.

```
// users.routes.ts

export const USERS_ROUTES: Routes = [

  { path: '', component: UserListComponent },

  { path: ':id', component: UserDetailComponent }

];
```

Then load them lazily in `app.routes.ts`:

```
{

  path: 'users',

  loadChildren: () =>
import('./users/users.routes').then(m =>
m.USERS_ROUTES)

}
```

If you're defining route-level providers or guards, keep them in the same file or co-located within the feature directory.

Testing Structure

Your `.spec.ts` test files should always sit **next to** the component/service they are testing. This keeps the test logic visible and tied to the code it verifies.

Example:

user-form.component.ts

user-form.component.spec.ts

This proximity:

Encourages writing tests alongside features.

Prevents stale or orphaned test files.

Makes test discovery easy during reviews or debugging.

If you're writing integration tests for routes or modules, place them in a `__tests__/` subfolder within the feature.

Environment-Specific Configurations

Configuration files such as `environment.ts` and `environment.prod.ts` should stay in `/src/environments/`. Never hardcode values like API base URLs, version info, or keys inside components or services.

Use centralized constants like:

```
export const environment = {

  apiUrl: 'https://api.dev.example.com',

  production: false

};
```

Access it from services:

```
import { environment } from
'@app/environments/environment';

this.http.get(`${environment.apiUrl}/users`);
```

This keeps logic consistent and environment switching effortless during builds.

A well-organized codebase lets you focus on solving business problems rather than hunting for files or deciphering naming logic. It makes your app accessible to new developers, more maintainable for existing ones, and ready to scale into something much larger with ease.

Configuring Environments and Constants

In any non-trivial Angular application, you'll encounter the need to work with **environment-specific settings**—things like API base URLs, feature flags, build modes, analytics tokens, or service endpoints that vary between development, staging, and production environments.

Angular offers a built-in system to handle environment configuration cleanly and predictably. It allows you to define constants that are automatically swapped depending on the build configuration, ensuring your application runs with the correct settings for each target context—without you having to manually change code.

Understanding Angular's Environment Configuration System

Angular uses a simple but powerful mechanism: during the build process, it **replaces** a default file (`environment.ts`) with a target-specific file (like `environment.prod.ts`) depending on the build configuration set in `angular.json`.

This is the official way to manage values that vary across deployment environments.

Your project should already include a basic setup under:

```
/src/environments/
    ├── environment.ts          ← used during development
    ├── environment.prod.ts     ← used during production build
```

The default development file might look like this:

```
// environment.ts

export const environment = {

  production: false,

  apiUrl: 'http://localhost:3000/api',

  enableDebugTools: true

};
```

For production:

```
// environment.prod.ts
export const environment = {
  production: true,
  apiUrl: 'https://api.myapp.com',
  enableDebugTools: false
};
```

Now, in your app, you can import this `environment` object wherever needed:

```
import { environment } from
'@app/environments/environment';

this.http.get(`${environment.apiUrl}/users`);
```

At build time, Angular will substitute the appropriate file, ensuring no production code points to local URLs or development toggles.

How Build File Replacement Works

In your `angular.json` file, under the `build.configurations` section, file replacements are defined like this:

```
"fileReplacements": [
  {
    "replace": "src/environments/environment.ts",
    "with": "src/environments/environment.prod.ts"
  }
]
```

So when you run:

`ng build --configuration production`

The `environment.prod.ts` file **replaces** `environment.ts`. You don't change your import paths; the tooling handles everything behind the scenes.

Adding More Environments

You're not limited to just `development` and `production`. You can add custom environments like `staging`, `testing`, or `preview`.

Create a new file:
`/src/environments/environment.staging.ts`

```
export const environment = {

  production: true,

  apiUrl: 'https://staging-api.myapp.com',

  enableDebugTools: false,

  sentryDsn: 'STAGING_SENTRY_DSN'

};
```

Add a new configuration in `angular.json`:

```
"configurations": {
  "staging": {
    "fileReplacements": [
      {
        "replace":
"src/environments/environment.ts",
        "with":
"src/environments/environment.staging.ts"
      }
    ],
    ...
  }
}
```

Build with:

ng build --configuration staging

You now have environment-specific settings for any deployment target.

Organizing Constants Cleanly

Not everything belongs in `environment.ts`. Use it only for **deployment-level settings**—values that differ between environments and need to be compiled in.

For values that are **constant across environments**, define them in a separate file such as:

`/src/app/constants/app.constants.ts`

```
export const APP_NAME = 'Customer Portal';
export const DEFAULT_PAGE_SIZE = 20;
export const SUPPORTED_LANGUAGES = ['en', 'fr',
'de'];
```

Then import as needed:

```
import { APP_NAME } from
'@app/constants/app.constants';
```

This separation keeps your environment files focused and reduces risk when updating code.

Accessing Environment Config in Services

A best practice is to inject environment config through a service, so components don't directly depend on environment structure.

```
@Injectable({ providedIn: 'root' })
export class ConfigService {
  readonly isProd = environment.production;
  readonly baseUrl = environment.apiUrl;
  readonly enableDebugTools =
environment.enableDebugTools;
}
```

Then in your component:

```
constructor(private config: ConfigService) {}

ngOnInit() {
  if (this.config.enableDebugTools) {
    console.log('Debug mode is ON');
  }
}
```

This pattern:

Centralizes access to environment values

Improves testability

Simplifies future refactoring

Security Warning: Never Store Secrets in Environment Files

Angular's environment files are part of the **frontend bundle**. They are fully exposed to the browser. Do not place API keys, database credentials, or anything sensitive inside them.

If you need to work with sensitive data, move it to a **secure backend service**. Your Angular app can request tokens or signed URLs from there. For example, never do this:

```
// ✗ Don't do this!

s3SecretAccessKey: 'abc123',

jwtSecret: 'top-secret-key'
```

Using Environment Flags for Conditional Logic

Use `environment.production` for enabling or disabling features:

```
if (environment.production) {

  enableProdMode();

}
```

Or conditionally show debug logs:

```
if (!environment.production &&
environment.enableDebugTools) {
  console.log('Debug info:', data);
}
```

This prevents debug code from leaking into production environments.

Versioning and Build Metadata

You can inject build metadata using Angular's CLI and define it in `environment.ts`.

Add a script in `package.json`:

```
"scripts": {
  "postbuild": "node ./scripts/generate-build-
info.js"
}
```

Then in `generate-build-info.js`:

```
const fs = require('fs');
const version = require('../package.json').version;
const commit =
require('child_process').execSync('git rev-parse
HEAD').toString().trim();

const content = `export const BUILD = {
  version: '${version}',
  commit: '${commit}',
  date: '${new Date().toISOString()}'
};`;

fs.writeFileSync('src/environments/build.ts',
content);
```

Now you can import this BUILD constant and show app version, commit hash, or build date in your UI:

```
import { BUILD } from '@app/environments/build';

console.log(`App Version: ${BUILD.version}
(${BUILD.date})`);
```

This adds traceability and transparency, especially in enterprise deployments.

Angular's environment system gives you a safe, flexible way to manage values that change between build contexts—without touching code. By structuring environment files clearly, using constants and services to centralize access, and avoiding risky practices like storing secrets on the client, you ensure that your application stays maintainable, predictable, and secure.

Chapter 8: Optimizing Performance in Angular Apps

Performance in Angular is not an afterthought—it's a foundational part of the framework's design. But building a fast Angular app still requires intentional choices. Whether it's about reducing unnecessary change detection cycles, trimming bundle size, or eliminating slow runtime bottlenecks, Angular gives you several powerful tools to keep your application lean, responsive, and efficient.

Change Detection Strategies and the New Signal System

At the heart of Angular's component architecture is a system that ensures the UI stays in sync with your application state. This system is called **change detection**. Every time something happens—whether it's user input, an HTTP response, a timer, or a state change—Angular needs to determine what part of the UI needs to be updated.

The way Angular does this is highly efficient by design, but in large applications or performance-critical views, it's crucial to understand how to **control and optimize change detection** rather than rely on defaults. Angular 19.2 offers both the traditional `ChangeDetectionStrategy` mechanisms and a new, fine-grained, declarative system based on **Signals**.

How Angular's Default Change Detection Works

Angular uses a zone-based system powered by the `zone.js` library. It patches asynchronous operations like `setTimeout`, `Promise`, and DOM events. When any of these operations finish, Angular triggers a global update cycle where it walks through the entire component tree and runs change detection on each component.

Here's what happens, by default:

The root component and all its children are checked recursively.

Angular compares the template values (what it renders) to the component's current state (what's in memory).

If anything has changed, the DOM is updated.

This is reliable and consistent—but not always the most efficient. As your app scales, traversing every component on every user interaction can become wasteful.

Improving Performance with OnPush Strategy

Angular gives you an alternate change detection strategy: `ChangeDetectionStrategy.OnPush`. With this, Angular will only check a component **if one of its @Input() properties has changed**, or if a reactive signal or observable inside it emits a new value.

To use it, set it in your component decorator:

```
import { ChangeDetectionStrategy, Component, Input
} from '@angular/core';

@Component({
  selector: 'app-profile-card',
  templateUrl: './profile-card.component.html',
  changeDetection: ChangeDetectionStrategy.OnPush
})
export class ProfileCardComponent {
  @Input() user!: User;
}
```

With this change:

Angular **skips** checking this component unless one of its inputs has changed.

Any change triggered inside child components **won't** cause Angular to re-check this component.

This reduces the frequency and depth of component tree traversals.

For `OnPush` to be effective, your component inputs need to be **immutable or reference-safe**—that is, they should change via assignment rather than mutation.

Common Pitfall with OnPush

Here's a problem to avoid:

```
this.user.name = 'Updated'; // mutation: Angular
may not detect this
```

Instead:

```
this.user = { ...this.user, name: 'Updated' }; //
reassignment: triggers detection
```

This reassignment creates a new object reference, which OnPush recognizes as a valid input change.

The Role of Signals in Angular 19.2

Angular 16 introduced **Signals**, and by 19.2, they are fully integrated into Angular's reactivity model. Signals are **change-aware state containers**. They tell Angular exactly when a value changes, so Angular doesn't need to guess or scan the whole tree.

A signal is a function that holds a value and notifies dependent code when it changes.

```
import { signal } from '@angular/core';

const count = signal(0);

count();          // get value → 0
count.set(5);     // update value → notifies any
bindings or computations
```

Signals allow you to **eliminate redundant change detection**, because Angular listens only to specific updates rather than relying on zones or global sweeps.

Using Signals in Components

Here's a complete example:

```
import { Component, signal } from '@angular/core';

@Component({
  selector: 'app-counter',
  standalone: true,
  template: `
```

```
    <h2>Count: {{ count() }}</h2>
    <button (click)="increment()">+1</button>
  `
})
export class CounterComponent {
  count = signal(0);

  increment() {
    this.count.set(this.count() + 1);
  }
}
```

Key benefits:

There's no need for `ChangeDetectorRef.markForCheck()` or `NgZone.run()`.

Signals automatically trigger UI updates in the exact place they are used.

Works perfectly with `OnPush` or standalone components.

Creating Derived Signals with `computed()`

You can create **derived values** using `computed()`:

```
import { computed } from '@angular/core';

const first = signal('Ada');
const last = signal('Lovelace');

const fullName = computed(() => `${first()}
${last()}`);
```

Angular automatically tracks dependencies here. If either `first` or `last` changes, `fullName` will re-evaluate.

Use `computed()` in components to build reactive template data without subscribing manually to observables or juggling state.

Side Effects and Reactions with `effect()`

To respond to changes without rendering, use `effect()`:

```
import { effect } from '@angular/core';
```

```
effect(() => {
  console.log('Counter updated:', count());
});
```

Use this in services or component logic to:

Trigger network requests

Log metrics

Mutate external state

This is Angular's alternative to `ngOnChanges` and subscriptions—it's cleaner, scoped, and reactive by default.

Signals vs Observables

Angular still fully supports observables via `RxJS`. But signals are built for:

View-bound state

Template reactivity

Fine-grained rendering

Use **signals** for local UI state, derived values, and user interactions.

Use **observables** for:

Async data (HTTP calls, WebSockets)

Streams of events (scroll, key presses, user input)

Complex pipelines with `map()`, `filter()`, etc.

You can bridge between them easily:

```
import { toSignal } from '@angular/core/rxjs-
interop';

const user$ = this.http.get<User>('/api/user');
const userSignal = toSignal(user$);
```

This lets you reuse observable-based APIs while integrating cleanly into signal-driven UIs.

Real-World Scenario: Performance in a Data-Heavy Grid

Suppose you're building a paginated table that displays hundreds of rows. Without optimization, every page change could trigger change detection across all cells.

With `OnPush` + Signals:

Each row can be its own standalone component.

The current page data is managed by a `signal()` in the parent.

Each cell accesses only its relevant row data via signal.

Updates (e.g., toggling a flag in a row) are scoped to that row, not the entire table.

This dramatically reduces the number of components Angular checks per event—from hundreds down to one or two.

Debugging Change Detection

Use **Angular DevTools** to inspect:

When components re-render

What triggers signal updates

Which inputs changed

It also helps you identify unnecessary renders and detect `Default` strategy components that could benefit from `OnPush`.

Angular's change detection is robust out of the box, but to scale your application effectively, you need to **take control** of it. Using `ChangeDetectionStrategy.OnPush` ensures Angular only checks what's necessary. The new **Signal system** takes it further, allowing your app to react to state changes with surgical precision—no zones, no subscriptions, no extra triggers.

Together, these tools give you complete control over performance-critical paths in your app. You render only what's needed, avoid unnecessary cycles, and keep your UI consistently responsive.

Ahead-of-Time (AOT) Compilation and Tree Shaking

When building Angular applications for production, two techniques play a central role in optimizing performance: **Ahead-of-Time (AOT) compilation** and **tree shaking**. These processes work together to shrink the size of your final JavaScript bundle, reduce parsing time in the browser, and eliminate dead code paths from your application.

Angular applications are made up of components and templates. The templates contain HTML and Angular-specific syntax like `*ngFor`, `{{ value }}`, and `[(ngModel)]`. In development, Angular can compile these templates in the browser at runtime—this is called **Just-in-Time (JIT)** compilation.

But in production, relying on JIT means:

Extra JavaScript code must be shipped with the app.

Template parsing and compiling happen in the browser.

Errors can appear at runtime instead of during build.

Ahead-of-Time (AOT) compilation solves this by moving template compilation to build time. Angular compiles your HTML templates into highly optimized JavaScript instructions **before** they are shipped to the browser.

This offers several advantages:

Faster startup time (no runtime template compilation).

Smaller bundles (no template compiler in the final code).

Early error detection (invalid bindings are caught at build).

Better optimization and minification by the bundler.

Enabling AOT Compilation

Angular CLI enables AOT by default in production builds. When you run:

```
ng build --configuration production
```

The CLI:

Enables AOT compilation.

Runs build optimizations and tree shaking.

Applies minification, compression, and source map generation.

There's no additional setup needed.

If you want to explicitly enable AOT during a non-production build:

```
ng build --aot
```

To verify that AOT is working, inspect your compiled component files in dist/. You won't find template strings. Instead, you'll see precompiled ɵcmp metadata and rendering instructions.

How AOT Compilation Improves Load Time

Let's walk through a simplified comparison.

JIT:

```
@Component({
  selector: 'app-greeting',
  template: `<p>Hello {{ name }}</p>`
})
export class GreetingComponent {
  name = 'Alice';
}
```

Under JIT:

The template is stored as a raw string.

At runtime, Angular parses and compiles the string.

The compiled view is then rendered.

AOT:

With AOT, the compiler turns the template into static rendering instructions like:

```
ɵɵtextInterpolate1('Hello ', ctx.name, '');
```

These instructions are:

Ready-to-execute JavaScript.

Tree-shakable (unused bindings are removed).

Optimized for rendering speed.

There's no string parsing or dynamic evaluation in the browser. The browser can render immediately.

What is Tree Shaking?

Tree shaking is the process of **removing unused code** from your final JavaScript bundle. The term comes from the idea of "shaking" a tree and letting dead leaves fall—unused exports are eliminated, resulting in smaller, faster-loading code.

Angular uses **ES modules** (`import` and `export`) to make this possible, and the CLI build pipeline (based on Webpack) supports tree shaking natively.

How Tree Shaking Works in Angular

Suppose you have a utility file like this:

```
export function generateUUID() { ... }

export function flattenArray(arr: any[]) { ... }

export function deepClone(obj: any) { ... }
```

If you import only `generateUUID()`:

```
import { generateUUID } from './utils';
```

And the other functions are never referenced in your app, the build process will remove them entirely from the output JavaScript bundle.

This works best when:

Each function, component, or service is defined in its own module.

You use ES module syntax (`import`/`export`) instead of CommonJS.

You avoid importing large libraries unless you need them.

Practical Tips for Better Tree Shaking

1. Avoid Side Effects in Modules

Tree shaking doesn't work if a module has side effects—even if its exports aren't used.

Bad example:

```
// utils.ts

console.log('Utils module loaded'); // prevents
tree shaking
```

Good example:

```
export function isEmail(value: string) {

  return value.includes('@');

}
```

2. Use Direct Imports, Not Namespace Imports

Don't do:

```
import * as _ from 'lodash';
```

This includes the entire library.

Do this instead:

```
import debounce from 'lodash/debounce';
```

3. Avoid Re-exporting Everything from Barrel Files (when unused)

Be selective when using `index.ts` to re-export. Re-exporting everything can keep unused symbols alive in the bundle.

4. Use `providedIn: 'root'` in Services

Angular removes unused services at build time if they are never injected.

```
@Injectable({ providedIn: 'root' })
export class DebugService { ... }
```

If no component or service injects `DebugService`, it is removed entirely from the final build.

Real-World Benefit

Let's say your development bundle is ~2MB. With AOT and tree shaking properly configured:

You could trim 500KB to 1MB by eliminating template compiler code.

You remove services, components, or modules that are never imported.

Lazy loaded routes and components are split into separate chunks that load only when needed.

This reduces:

Initial page load time

Memory usage

Time to interactive (TTI)

Especially on mobile devices or slow networks, this translates directly into better user experience and higher engagement.

Validating Tree Shaking and AOT Output

Use this command to analyze your bundle:

```
ng build --stats-json
```

Then install and run Webpack Bundle Analyzer:

```
npx webpack-bundle-analyzer dist/browser/stats.json
```

This gives you a visual breakdown of what's in your bundle—so you can track down unused libraries, oversized modules, or leaks in lazy loading.

Ahead-of-Time compilation and tree shaking are not optional extras—they are critical to producing fast, production-ready Angular applications. AOT moves expensive work from the browser to the build process. Tree shaking eliminates dead code, trims libraries, and helps your users load less, wait less, and interact faster.

Lazy Loading and Code Splitting

One of the most effective ways to optimize an Angular application's startup performance is to **avoid loading everything at once**. As your app grows, so does its JavaScript bundle size. If you ship the entire codebase to every user up front—whether they need all of it or not—you waste bandwidth, slow down the time to interactive, and degrade the overall experience.

This is where **lazy loading** and **code splitting** come in. These techniques allow Angular to load only what the user needs, when they need it. Instead of bundling the whole app into one massive JavaScript file, Angular splits it into smaller chunks. Each chunk contains just enough logic to handle the current route or feature. The rest stays on the server until it's requested.

Angular provides built-in support for lazy loading at the routing level, and it complements this with Webpack-based automatic code splitting during the build process. When combined correctly, you get a fast initial load and a snappy user experience throughout your app.

Why Lazy Loading Matters

Without lazy loading, Angular builds a single `main.js` bundle that contains everything—components, modules, services, third-party libraries, and internal utilities. This becomes problematic in applications with:

Multiple independent features

Administrative or reporting sections accessed only by a few users

Rarely visited routes like Settings, Help, or Privacy Policy

Embedded analytics dashboards or rich visualizations

Lazy loading ensures these parts of the app are excluded from the initial bundle and loaded **only when the route is accessed**.

This means:

Faster first-page load (smaller main bundle)

Reduced memory usage

Better Lighthouse scores

Efficient use of network resources, especially on mobile

Lazy Loading Standalone Components with Angular 15+

In modern Angular (15 and above), where standalone components are the default, lazy loading becomes even simpler and cleaner.

Let's say you have a `SettingsComponent` that you want to load lazily.

```
// settings.component.ts

@Component({

  selector: 'app-settings',

  standalone: true,

  template: `<h2>Settings Page</h2>`

})

export class SettingsComponent {}
```

Then in your route configuration:

```
const routes: Routes = [
  {
    path: 'settings',
    loadComponent: () =>

import('./settings/settings.component').then(m =>
m.SettingsComponent)
  }
];
```

With this setup:

The Angular router creates a new chunk for `settings.component.ts`.

The component and any dependencies (e.g., forms, services) are bundled separately.

This chunk is loaded asynchronously when the user visits `/settings`.

This pattern is ideal for isolated screens or feature pages.

Lazy Loading Feature Routes

If you're building a larger feature that includes multiple components and its own routing configuration, lazy loading the entire feature route is the better approach.

Let's say you have a feature directory:

/src/app/admin/

> ├── **admin-dashboard.component.ts**
>
> ├── **user-management.component.ts**
>
> ├── **admin.routes.ts**

Define the routes:

```
export const ADMIN_ROUTES: Routes = [

  { path: '', component: AdminDashboardComponent },

  { path: 'users', component:
UserManagementComponent }

];
```

Then lazy-load it from your main routes:

```
const routes: Routes = [
  {
    path: 'admin',
    loadChildren: () =>
      import('./admin/admin.routes').then(m =>
m.ADMIN_ROUTES)
  }
];
```

Angular will:

Create a chunk containing all components in the admin feature

Load this chunk only when the user navigates to `/admin`

Keep it cached in memory during the session unless configured otherwise

This is ideal for user-specific features like dashboards, analytics, or content management.

Using Route-Level Providers with Lazy Loading

You can scope services to lazy-loaded routes to ensure they're not part of the initial bundle.

```
export const REPORTS_ROUTES: Routes = [
  {
    path: '',
    component: ReportsComponent,
    providers: [ReportsService]
  }
];
```

This keeps `ReportsService` out of the global injector and ensures it's instantiated only when `/reports` is active.

Scoping providers this way enhances both performance and encapsulation.

Splitting by Component, Not Just Routes

Sometimes, a large reusable component—like a chart, visual editor, or markdown renderer—shouldn't be included in your main bundle, even if it's not route-based.

You can load such components dynamically using `loadComponent()` with `NgIf` or similar logic:

```
@Component({
  selector: 'app-lazy-chart-loader',
  standalone: true,
  template: `
    <button (click)="load()">Show Chart</button>
    <ng-container *ngIf="chartComponent">
      <ng-container
*ngComponentOutlet="chartComponent"></ng-container>
    </ng-container>
  `
})
export class LazyChartLoaderComponent {
  chartComponent: Type<any> | null = null;
```

```
  async load() {
    const module = await
import('./chart/chart.component');
    this.chartComponent = module.ChartComponent;
  }
}
```

The chart component's code will only be downloaded when the user clicks "Show Chart". This technique is ideal for resource-intensive UI widgets.

Understanding Code Splitting with Webpack

Angular CLI uses Webpack under the hood. Webpack automatically creates **chunks** for lazy-loaded components and modules. These chunks are identified using numeric or hashed filenames like `settings-settings-component.[hash].js`.

You can inspect chunk usage with:

```
ng build --configuration production --stats-json

npx webpack-bundle-analyzer dist/browser/stats.json
```

This tool shows:

The size of each chunk

What components and libraries are included

Opportunities for refactoring or optimization

Aim to:

Keep the initial bundle (`main.js`) as small as possible

Bundle related features into coherent chunks

Avoid loading large libraries globally if used in one route only

Real-World Scenario: Optimizing a Customer Portal

Let's say you're building a B2B customer portal. The app has:

A product catalog (`/products`)

An order history page (/orders)

An administrative panel (/admin)

A settings page (/settings)

You lazy load everything except the home and product routes, which are accessed most frequently.

```
const routes: Routes = [
  { path: '', component: HomeComponent },
  { path: 'products', component:
ProductListComponent },
  {
    path: 'orders',
    loadChildren: () =>
import('./orders/orders.routes').then(m =>
m.ORDERS_ROUTES)
  },
  {
    path: 'admin',
    loadChildren: () =>
import('./admin/admin.routes').then(m =>
m.ADMIN_ROUTES)
  },
  {
    path: 'settings',
    loadComponent: () =>
import('./settings/settings.component').then(m =>
m.SettingsComponent)
  }
];
```

The result:

The initial bundle contains only Home and Product features.

Admin and Settings are split into separate bundles.

The app loads fast and doesn't load unnecessary logic until needed.

Best Practices for Lazy Loading and Code Splitting

Start with feature-based route splitting first.

Use `loadComponent()` for pages or modals not part of a feature set.

Avoid importing lazily-loaded services or components in eagerly-loaded modules.

Keep shared modules slim—don't accidentally re-import entire features.

Use route-level providers for isolated service logic.

Regularly analyze your build with `webpack-bundle-analyzer`.

Lazy loading and code splitting aren't about complexity—they're about **precision**. Instead of assuming that every user will touch every part of your app, Angular allows you to send only the pieces that are relevant to each interaction. When used well, these techniques make your app feel fast, scalable, and responsive.

Whether you're optimizing for first-page load on mobile or keeping memory usage down on complex enterprise dashboards, Angular's support for lazy loading and granular code splitting ensures you never have to choose between performance and flexibility.

Runtime Debugging with Angular DevTools

When you're working on a complex Angular application, being able to understand what's happening in the browser at runtime is critical. Angular DevTools gives you real-time visibility into how your application behaves—from component rendering and signal updates to routing transitions and change detection cycles.

This tool is not just for finding bugs. It's for optimizing rendering, tracking signal reactivity, ensuring efficient component tree updates, and debugging input bindings and services—all without modifying your codebase or flooding the console with logs.

Installing Angular DevTools

Angular DevTools is a browser extension available for Chrome and Firefox. You can install it directly from the Chrome Web Store or Firefox Add-ons:

Angular DevTools for Chrome

Angular DevTools for Firefox

After installation:

Open your Angular application in development mode (`ng serve`).

Open your browser's Developer Tools.

You'll see a new "Angular" tab.

If you don't see it:

Ensure you're running a development build.

Confirm the app uses Angular 12 or newer (19.2 fully supported).

Make sure Angular's `enableProdMode()` hasn't been called.

Angular DevTools won't attach to production builds because those are optimized, tree-shaken, and minified—stripping metadata needed for inspection.

Understanding the Angular Tab

Once Angular DevTools attaches to your app, you'll see a UI that is split into a few core panels:

1. Component Tree

This is the visual hierarchy of all components currently rendered in the application. You can:

Inspect component names and structure.

Click on any component to view its **inputs**, **outputs**, and **state**.

View signals or injected services used within the component.

Each node shows:

The component selector

Its active `@Input()` properties

Any `@Output()` bindings

Signal values used in the template

Use case: You select a button component and instantly see the current value of @Input() label, without writing a single console.log.

2. Signal Explorer

This panel becomes available when your app uses Angular Signals.

Here you can:

View all defined signals in scope.

See their current values.

Inspect which components or computed values depend on them.

Monitor when and why a signal was updated.

Example:

If you have:

```
count = signal(0);
```

The signal explorer shows:

```
count: 0
```

Updated when: Button click → increment()

If another signal or computed value depends on count, you can trace how the update flowed through the application.

3. Change Detection Profiler

This panel lets you measure:

How long change detection takes per cycle.

Which components were updated.

Whether updates were caused by signals, inputs, or zone-triggered changes.

Start profiling:

Click **Start Profiling**.

Interact with your app.

Click **Stop Profiling**.

You'll see a timeline and a breakdown by component.

Use case: You're diagnosing a slow list component. Profiling reveals that a parent component without `OnPush` is causing unnecessary full-tree updates. You then refactor it to use `ChangeDetectionStrategy.OnPush`.

4. Router Explorer

If you're using Angular Router, this panel shows:

Current route path and parameters.

Route tree structure.

Activated outlets.

Guards and resolvers associated with each route.

Navigation history.

Use case: You navigate to `/products/42`, and DevTools confirms:

ProductDetailComponent is active.

Route param `id` is `42`.

canActivate: [AuthGuard] was executed.

You get instant feedback on which guards passed, what route-level providers were used, and what the router's internal state is at any moment.

5. Injector Graph and Providers

You can inspect what services are available in the current injector context:

App-wide (root injector)

Route-scoped

Component-scoped

DevTools lets you:

View the full hierarchy of injectors.

Understand where services are provided and how they cascade.

Detect if multiple instances of a service are unexpectedly created.

This is helpful when debugging issues related to provider scope—such as when a service doesn't maintain shared state due to being scoped too narrowly.

Live Editing Inputs and Signals

One powerful feature in DevTools is the ability to **edit values directly**.

In the component panel:

Click on an input value or a signal.

Modify it and press enter.

Angular updates the UI immediately, just as if the input had changed from inside the app.

Example: Your `UserProfileComponent` has an input `userId` = 23. You change it to 42, and the component reloads user 42's details.

This is great for debugging component rendering logic or validating edge cases without needing to build UI tools for manual input.

Debugging Component Update Issues

Use Angular DevTools to diagnose:

Components that update too frequently (caused by lack of `OnPush`).

Inputs not updating due to incorrect object mutation.

Signals not triggering updates because the reactive function was never accessed.

Guards not firing due to incorrect router configuration.

By inspecting bindings and change detection timings visually, you move faster than traditional console-based debugging.

How DevTools Supports Standalone Components

If you're building with standalone components, Angular DevTools displays them with equal clarity:

You don't need to register them in a module for DevTools to recognize them.

Signals, effects, and computed values used inside standalone components appear just as they do in traditional setups.

Route-level and component-level scoped providers are visible and inspectable.

This keeps the debugging experience consistent even as Angular evolves away from traditional `NgModules`.

Performance Impact

Angular DevTools is lightweight and does not slow down your app under normal usage. However:

Keep in mind it attaches only in development mode.

Don't ship apps with DevTools enabled—production builds automatically exclude it.

For performance-critical scenarios, use the profiler to understand the runtime cost of change detection, especially on mobile or constrained hardware.

Real-World Example: Diagnosing an Infinite Render Loop

In one case, a developer accidentally wrote:

```
this.counter.set(this.counter() + 1);
```

...inside a `computed()` block, which re-triggered itself infinitely.

With DevTools:

The signal explorer showed `counter` updating non-stop.

The change detection profiler revealed 100+ renders per second.

The developer quickly traced and fixed the infinite update.

This type of feedback loop can be difficult to catch by logs alone—but with real-time tooling, it becomes trivial.

Angular DevTools brings transparency and control to runtime behavior. You don't have to guess what triggered a re-render, which input caused a change, or why a signal didn't propagate. You can see it—all of it—in real time.

Use it every day:

When wiring up new signals or reactive state.

When optimizing component rendering.

When setting up or refactoring routing logic.

When debugging change detection inefficiencies.

The more complex your application, the more invaluable this tool becomes. Angular is built to scale—but tools like DevTools are what make that scalability **understandable** and **manageable** in practice.

Chapter 9: Testing and Debugging Angular Applications

Writing Angular code is only half the job—**verifying** that it behaves as expected is just as essential. Robust testing is what gives you the confidence to refactor fearlessly, ship faster, and catch regressions early. Debugging, on the other hand, is the art of quickly understanding and resolving issues that do make it into the codebase.

Angular supports a layered approach to testing:

Unit tests to validate isolated logic like components, services, and pipes.

Integration tests to simulate the interaction of components within an application context.

End-to-end (E2E) tests that simulate real user flows across pages and services.

Angular's CLI tooling, combined with TestBed, Jasmine, and modern E2E tools like Cypress, makes this workflow not only powerful but approachable. In this chapter, we'll walk through how to set up, write, and run tests at every level of your Angular app. You'll also learn how to debug your app systematically using console insights and browser tools.

Unit Testing Components, Services, and Pipes

Testing in Angular starts with units—the smallest possible pieces of functionality. A unit could be a component method, a service function, or a pipe transform. When you test a unit, you're verifying that it behaves correctly in complete isolation from the rest of the application.

Unit tests should be simple, fast, and precise. They give you the confidence that changes in one part of your code won't unexpectedly break something elsewhere. In Angular, you typically write unit tests using Jasmine as the test framework and run them with Karma or Jest, depending on your setup.

Unit Testing a Component with Inputs and Template Bindings

Suppose you're building a small user badge component that displays a user's name. It uses Angular's @Input() binding to receive data from its parent.

```
@Component({
  selector: 'app-user-badge',
  standalone: true,
  template: `<span class="username">{{ name
}}</span>`
})
export class UserBadgeComponent {
  @Input() name!: string;
}
```

Let's test that it displays the name correctly:

```
import { ComponentFixture, TestBed } from
'@angular/core/testing';
import { UserBadgeComponent } from './user-
badge.component';

describe('UserBadgeComponent', () => {
  let fixture:
ComponentFixture<UserBadgeComponent>;

  beforeEach(() => {
    TestBed.configureTestingModule({
      imports: [UserBadgeComponent]
    });

    fixture =
TestBed.createComponent(UserBadgeComponent);
  });

  it('should render the user name', () => {
    fixture.componentInstance.name = 'Ada
Lovelace';
    fixture.detectChanges(); // triggers Angular's
change detection

    const element: HTMLElement =
fixture.nativeElement;
```

```
    const username =
element.querySelector('.username')?.textContent?.tr
im();
    expect(username).toBe('Ada Lovelace');
  });
});
```

Explanation:

We manually set the `@Input()` value (name) before change detection.

We trigger the update using `fixture.detectChanges()`.

Then, we read the rendered DOM and assert it contains the correct text.

This test verifies both the input binding and the template interpolation.

Unit Testing a Service

Services are pure business logic. They're not tied to the DOM, which makes them perfect for isolated testing. Here's a basic example:

```
@Injectable({ providedIn: 'root' })
export class CalculatorService {
  add(a: number, b: number): number {
    return a + b;
  }

  divide(a: number, b: number): number {
    if (b === 0) throw new Error('Division by
zero');
    return a / b;
  }
}
```

The test for this service is straightforward:

```
import { TestBed } from '@angular/core/testing';
import { CalculatorService } from
'./calculator.service';

describe('CalculatorService', () => {
  let service: CalculatorService;
```

```
  beforeEach(() => {
    TestBed.configureTestingModule({});
    service = TestBed.inject(CalculatorService);
  });

  it('should add two numbers', () => {
    expect(service.add(3, 4)).toBe(7);
  });

  it('should divide two numbers correctly', () => {
    expect(service.divide(10, 2)).toBe(5);
  });

  it('should throw error when dividing by zero', ()
=> {
    expect(() => service.divide(5,
0)).toThrowError('Division by zero');
  });
});
```

This set of tests checks:

Normal behavior (`add` and `divide`)

Exception handling (`divide` with zero)

You can also use spies if your service calls external APIs or other dependencies you want to isolate.

Mocking Dependencies in Component Unit Tests

Sometimes, components rely on services. To test them independently, you mock the service to control its behavior.

Component:

```
@Component({
  selector: 'app-greeter',
  standalone: true,
  template: `<p>{{ greeting }}</p>`
})
export class GreeterComponent {
  greeting = '';
```

```
  constructor(private service: GreetingService) {}

  ngOnInit() {
    this.greeting = this.service.sayHello();
  }
}
```

Service:

```
@Injectable({ providedIn: 'root' })

export class GreetingService {

  sayHello(): string {

    return 'Hello World';

  }

}
```

Test with a mock:

```
class MockGreetingService {
  sayHello() {
    return 'Hi from mock';
  }
}

describe('GreeterComponent', () => {
  let fixture: ComponentFixture<GreeterComponent>;

  beforeEach(() => {
    TestBed.configureTestingModule({
      imports: [GreeterComponent],
      providers: [{ provide: GreetingService,
useClass: MockGreetingService }]
    });

    fixture =
TestBed.createComponent(GreeterComponent);
    fixture.detectChanges();
  });
```

```
  it('should display greeting from the mock
service', () => {
    const content =
fixture.nativeElement.querySelector('p')?.textConte
nt?.trim();
    expect(content).toBe('Hi from mock');
  });
});
```

This ensures that your component is tested **without relying on real service logic**, which may have its own issues or dependencies.

Unit Testing a Pipe

Pipes are easy to test because they are pure functions. Let's test a custom pipe that capitalizes words.

Pipe:

```
@Pipe({ name: 'capitalize' })
export class CapitalizePipe implements
PipeTransform {
  transform(value: string): string {
    return value.replace(/\b\w/g, char =>
char.toUpperCase());
  }
}
```

Test:

```
describe('CapitalizePipe', () => {
  const pipe = new CapitalizePipe();

  it('should capitalize each word', () => {
    const result = pipe.transform('hello angular
testing');
    expect(result).toBe('Hello Angular Testing');
  });

  it('should return empty string for empty input',
() => {
    expect(pipe.transform('')).toBe('');
  });
```

184

```
it('should handle null input gracefully', () => {
    expect(() => pipe.transform(null as
any)).toThrow();
  });
});
```

You're testing:

Core functionality

Edge cases

Error handling

If you want to allow null or undefined inputs gracefully, update the pipe and adjust your test accordingly.

Running Unit Tests

To run your tests using Angular CLI:

ng test

This launches the test runner (usually Karma) and watches for changes. It also displays results in the console and optionally in a browser.

If you're using Jest (common in modern setups), the command may look like:

npx jest

Angular supports both with minimal configuration changes.

Writing Effective Unit Tests: Guidelines

Test only one unit per test case.

Set up the minimal environment needed—avoid unnecessary modules or services.

Mock external dependencies.

Use descriptive names: it('should render the title', ...)

Keep your expectations explicit and focused.

Use `beforeEach()` only for setup shared across **all** test cases.

If a test fails, the cause should be obvious from the test body.

Unit tests are the first line of defense in an Angular project. They're fast, reliable, and essential for maintaining code quality. By writing clear, isolated tests for your components, services, and pipes, you ensure that the core logic of your application remains stable and predictable—even as new features are added.

Integration Testing and Test Bed Configuration

Unit tests are great for validating isolated logic. But as your application grows in complexity, it's just as important to test how different parts work together— how components render templates, how services respond to inputs, how forms validate across fields, and how multiple dependencies interact in a real Angular context.

That's where **integration testing** comes in. In Angular, you write integration tests using the same testing infrastructure—Jasmine or Jest with Angular's `TestBed` utility—but instead of mocking or isolating everything, you allow components, templates, and services to function together, much like they do at runtime.

Integration tests validate **the collaboration** between multiple pieces of logic. This includes:

Components and their templates

Services injected into those components

Forms and validators

Child components and `@Input()`/`@Output()` bindings

Pipes or directives applied in the view

Unlike unit tests, you don't mock away the template, the DOM, or the service logic. Instead, you render everything using Angular's change detection system and test the actual output and behavior.

Angular provides `TestBed` for this purpose—it lets you compile components in a simulated Angular application context.

Understanding and Using TestBed

The `TestBed` utility is Angular's primary testing harness. It allows you to:

Compile components, including their HTML templates

Inject services into those components

Render components in a test fixture

Trigger change detection manually

Simulate DOM events

Let's begin with a simple component that integrates form control, a service call, and DOM rendering.

Example: LoginComponent with Reactive Forms

Here's the component:

```
@Component({
  selector: 'app-login',
  standalone: true,
  imports: [CommonModule, ReactiveFormsModule],
  template: `
    <form [formGroup]="form" (ngSubmit)="submit()">
      <input formControlName="email" />
      <input formControlName="password"
type="password" />
      <button type="submit">Login</button>
    </form>
    <p class="error" *ngIf="error">{{ error }}</p>
  `
})
export class LoginComponent {
  form = new FormGroup({
    email: new FormControl('',
[Validators.required, Validators.email]),
    password: new FormControl('',
Validators.required)
  });
```

```
  error = '';

  constructor(private auth: AuthService) {}

  submit() {
    if (this.form.valid) {
      const { email, password } = this.form.value;
      this.auth.login(email, password).subscribe({
        error: () => (this.error = 'Login failed')
      });
    }
  }
}
```

Now let's test the **integration** between:

The form

The DOM

The **AuthService**

Mocking the Service for Integration Testing

We don't need the real HTTP call—we want to test the interaction. So we'll **mock** AuthService but keep the rest of the component logic and DOM intact.

```
class MockAuthService {
  login(email: string, password: string):
Observable<any> {
    if (email === 'fail@test.com') {
      return throwError(() => new Error('Invalid
credentials'));
    }
    return of({ token: 'abc123' });
  }
}
```

Setting Up TestBed with a Standalone Component

```
describe('LoginComponent (integration test)', () =>
{
  let fixture: ComponentFixture<LoginComponent>;
```

```
  let component: LoginComponent;

  beforeEach(async () => {
    await TestBed.configureTestingModule({
      imports: [LoginComponent],
      providers: [{ provide: AuthService, useClass:
MockAuthService }]
    }).compileComponents();

    fixture =
TestBed.createComponent(LoginComponent);
    component = fixture.componentInstance;
    fixture.detectChanges();
  });

  it('should render form with two inputs and one
button', () => {
    const element: HTMLElement =
fixture.nativeElement;
    const inputs =
element.querySelectorAll('input');
    const button = element.querySelector('button');

    expect(inputs.length).toBe(2);

expect(button?.textContent?.trim()).toBe('Login');
  });

  it('should show error message on failed login',
fakeAsync(() => {
    component.form.setValue({ email:
'fail@test.com', password: 'wrong' });

fixture.debugElement.nativeElement.querySelector('f
orm').dispatchEvent(new Event('submit'));
    tick(); // simulate passage of time for async

    fixture.detectChanges();
    const error =
fixture.nativeElement.querySelector('.error')?.text
Content?.trim();
    expect(error).toBe('Login failed');
```

```
  }));
});
```

Key points:

The component is tested in its real structure (standalone, using actual form controls).

We simulate real browser events (`submit`) and check real DOM output.

The service call is mocked, but its integration with the component is intact.

We use `fakeAsync()` and `tick()` to resolve async observables without delays.

Triggering DOM Events

To simulate user behavior:

Use `dispatchEvent()` on native elements

Or use Angular's `DebugElement` with `triggerEventHandler`

Example:

```
fixture.debugElement.query(By.css('form')).triggerE
ventHandler('ngSubmit', {});
```

Always call `fixture.detectChanges()` afterward to ensure the template updates.

Testing Child Component Interaction

Suppose your component uses a child component like this:

```
<app-user-info [user]="user"></app-user-info>
```

If you're doing an integration test, you can:

Include the child component in `imports`

Or mock it using a stub

Stub component for integration testing:

```
@Component({
```

```
  selector: 'app-user-info',
  standalone: true,
  template: `<p>User Info</p>`
})
class StubUserInfoComponent {
  @Input() user!: any;
}
```

Then in your test:

```
await TestBed.configureTestingModule({

  imports: [MainComponent, StubUserInfoComponent]

}).compileComponents();
```

This way, you validate that:

The parent passes the right data to the child

The child component renders when expected

You're not testing the full behavior of the child, just that it's used correctly.

Testing Component-Directive-Pipe Integration

When testing components that use directives or pipes, include them in `imports` or mock them with stubs.

For instance, a component using `*ngIf` and a custom pipe would need:

imports: [CommonModule, MyCustomPipe]

This ensures the template compiles and behaves as expected in the test.

Testing Outputs and Events

If your component emits events via `@Output()`:

```
@Component({
  selector: 'app-confirm-button',
  standalone: true,
  template: `<button
(click)="confirm.emit()">Confirm</button>`
})
```

```
export class ConfirmButtonComponent {
  @Output() confirm = new EventEmitter<void>();
}
```

Test it like this:

```
it('should emit confirm event on click', () => {
  const fixture =
TestBed.createComponent(ConfirmButtonComponent);
  const component = fixture.componentInstance;

  spyOn(component.confirm, 'emit');
  fixture.detectChanges();


fixture.nativeElement.querySelector('button').click
();

  expect(component.confirm.emit).toHaveBeenCalled();
});
```

This confirms that template bindings and event outputs are wired correctly.

Integration testing is your bridge between isolated unit tests and full end-to-end automation. It verifies that your components, templates, forms, services, and child components actually work together—using real Angular change detection and DOM rendering.

End-to-End Testing with Cypress

End-to-end (E2E) testing is the closest you get to **how your users actually experience your Angular application**. Unlike unit or integration tests that run in memory, E2E tests spin up your application in a browser and interact with it like a real person would—clicking buttons, typing in inputs, navigating routes, submitting forms, and waiting for network responses. These tests validate that all parts of your app work together correctly, including the frontend, routing, authentication flows, and server communication.

For Angular applications, **Cypress** has become the preferred tool for E2E testing. It offers a fast, modern testing experience, complete with a visual test runner, real browser execution, automatic waiting, screenshot capture, video recording, and a clean, chainable syntax for writing readable tests.

Setting Up Cypress with Angular CLI

Cypress doesn't come bundled with Angular by default, but Angular CLI provides a schematic for installing and wiring it up.

Run:

`ng add @cypress/schematic`

This command:

Adds Cypress as a dev dependency.

Sets up the Cypress configuration files.

Replaces the default e2e builder in `angular.json` with Cypress.

Creates a `cypress/` directory with sample test specs and support files.

Now, to open Cypress:

`npx cypress open`

Or to run headlessly:

`npx cypress run`

This launches Cypress's interactive UI or command-line runner depending on your environment.

Basic Cypress Folder Structure

After setup, your project includes:

```
/cypress/
    ├── e2e/              ← test specs go here
    ├── support/          ← custom commands, test hooks
    └── fixtures/         ← mock data for tests
cypress.config.ts    ← Cypress configuration
```

Each file in the `e2e/` folder becomes a separate test suite. You can create one spec file per feature or page:

```
login.cy.ts

dashboard.cy.ts

settings.cy.ts
```

This keeps your E2E tests modular and easier to maintain.

Writing Your First Cypress Test

Let's write a simple test that:

Visits the login page.

Enters email and password.

Submits the form.

Verifies redirection to the dashboard.

```
describe('Login Flow', () => {
  it('logs in with valid credentials', () => {
    cy.visit('/login');


cy.get('input[formControlName="email"]').type('test
@example.com');

cy.get('input[formControlName="password"]').type('p
assword123');
    cy.get('button[type="submit"]').click();

    cy.url().should('include', '/dashboard');
    cy.contains('Welcome, Test User');
  });
});
```

This test is doing exactly what a user would:

Navigating to the page.

Typing in fields.

Clicking a button.

Checking that they landed on the right route and see expected content.

Cypress automatically waits for elements to appear—no need for `sleep` or `wait`.

Best Practices for Selectors

Avoid relying on brittle selectors like class names or tag names. Instead, use **data attributes** for test targeting:

```
<input data-cy="email" />

<button data-cy="login-button">Login</button>
```

Test code:

```
cy.get('[data-cy="email"]').type('admin@site.com');

cy.get('[data-cy="login-button"]').click();
```

Using `data-cy` attributes:

Prevents tests from breaking due to CSS changes.

Keeps your HTML semantically clean.

Makes your E2E tests resilient and easier to debug.

Mocking Backend API Responses

You don't always want your E2E tests to hit a real API—especially in CI environments. Cypress makes mocking easy with `cy.intercept()`.

Example:

```
cy.intercept('POST', '/api/login', {

  statusCode: 200,

  body: { token: 'fake-jwt', user: { name: 'Test User' } }

}).as('loginRequest');
```

You can combine this with test logic:

```
cy.get('[data-cy="email"]').type('user@test.com');
```

```
cy.get('[data-cy="password"]').type('123456');
cy.get('[data-cy="login-button"]').click();

cy.wait('@loginRequest');
cy.url().should('include', '/dashboard');
```

Mocking is ideal for:

Isolating frontend behavior

Testing edge cases and error states

Running repeatable tests across environments

You can even simulate failed requests:

```
cy.intercept('POST', '/api/login', {

  statusCode: 401,

  body: { message: 'Invalid credentials' }

});
```

Then assert that your app displays the error message.

Running Cypress in CI

To automate Cypress tests as part of your CI/CD pipeline, add this to your scripts:

```
"scripts": {

  "e2e": "cypress run"

}
```

Use a headless browser like Electron or Chrome:

npx cypress run --browser chrome

CI systems like GitHub Actions, GitLab CI, CircleCI, and Jenkins all support Cypress out of the box. You can also record video or screenshot failures:

npx cypress run --record --key <your-dashboard-key>

This gives you test visibility and playback logs in the Cypress dashboard (optional, free tier available).

Example: Testing a Product Search Flow

Let's say your Angular app includes a product search page:

User enters a term in the search box.

App sends an HTTP request to `/api/products?q=`....

Results are rendered as a list of cards.

Test:

```
describe('Product Search', () => {
  beforeEach(() => {
    cy.intercept('GET', '/api/products?q=keyboard',
{
      fixture: 'products/keyboard.json'
    }).as('searchRequest');
  });

  it('shows results when a term is entered', () =>
{
    cy.visit('/products');
    cy.get('[data-cy="search-
input"]').type('keyboard{enter}');
    cy.wait('@searchRequest');

    cy.get('[data-cy="product-
card"]').should('have.length', 3);
    cy.contains('Mechanical Keyboard');
  });
});
```

With **fixtures/products/keyboard.json:**

```
[

  { "id": 1, "name": "Mechanical Keyboard" },

  { "id": 2, "name": "Wireless Keyboard" },
```

```
  { "id": 3, "name": "Ergonomic Keyboard" }
]
```

This test verifies:

Input field behavior

Correct backend request

Rendering of real data

It doesn't rely on the actual API, so it's fast and deterministic.

Debugging Failed Cypress Tests

When a test fails, Cypress gives you:

The exact step where it failed.

A DOM snapshot at the time of failure.

A stack trace with full context.

Optional screenshot and video capture.

This is far more helpful than traditional console errors.

To make debugging easier:

Use `cy.log()` for custom step messages.

Use `.debug()` to pause at a step.

Use `.screenshot()` to capture custom states.

Structuring E2E Tests for Maintainability

Organize specs by feature (`login.cy.ts`, `profile.cy.ts`, etc.).

Use `fixtures/` to store reusable mock data.

Use `support/commands.ts` to create custom `cy.login()`, `cy.fillForm()`, etc.

Group tests with `describe()` and isolate cases with `it()`.

This reduces duplication and keeps your tests readable over time.

Cypress gives Angular developers a full-featured E2E solution that's fast, expressive, and designed for real web applications. With Cypress, you simulate what your users actually do—from logging in to submitting forms and navigating complex UI flows.

Use Cypress when you want to validate:

Route transitions

Authentication flows

Form validation with backend feedback

Component interactions across pages

Error handling and conditional UI

Cypress makes it easier to ship confidently—knowing that your application works, not just in theory, but in actual browser environments under real interaction scenarios.

Debugging Best Practices and Console Monitoring

Every developer encounters bugs. What separates efficient development from endless frustration is how systematically you approach debugging. Angular provides powerful tools—within the framework and through browser integrations—that allow you to trace, inspect, and understand exactly what's happening when your application doesn't behave as expected.

Before you start throwing `console.log` statements everywhere, slow down and define **what exactly is going wrong**. Ask yourself:

What behavior did I expect?

What did I observe instead?

When does it happen—on page load, after an interaction, or randomly?

Is it consistent or intermittent?

Is there any relevant user input, routing, service call, or signal update involved?

Answering these questions first helps you zoom in on **where to look**—in the template, the component logic, service layer, or data flow.

Use `console.log` with Purpose

Logging is the simplest and fastest form of debugging. But most developers use it poorly by logging vague, context-less values.

Weak log:

```
console.log('value', value);
```

Better:

```
console.log('[ProductService] fetchProducts
response:', value);
```

When logging errors, always include:

Source of the log (component or service name)

What the operation is

What inputs caused it

What the actual response or error was

Example:

```
this.http.get('/api/products').subscribe({

  next: res => console.log('[ProductService]
/products success:', res),

  error: err => console.error('[ProductService]
/products failed', err.message, err.status)

});
```

Always log **in full context** so that you don't need to cross-reference five files to understand what was being logged.

Avoid Overlogging in Production

Use Angular's built-in `environment.ts` configuration to toggle logs:

```
if (!environment.production) {
  console.log('[Debug] Form value:',
this.form.value);
}
```

Or better, abstract logging through a `LoggerService`:

```
@Injectable({ providedIn: 'root' })
export class LoggerService {
  log(message: string, ...optional: any[]) {
    if (!environment.production) {
      console.log(message, ...optional);
    }
  }
}
```

Use it consistently across services and components so that you can turn off all logs globally during production builds.

Use Angular DevTools for Runtime Inspection

Install Angular DevTools (covered previously in detail) and use it actively:

Inspect the component tree and see what inputs are being passed.

View signal state and derived computations.

Track router transitions and current params.

Measure which components are triggering change detection and how often.

Use case: You notice that a component is re-rendering more than expected. DevTools shows that it's using the `Default` change detection strategy and receives new object references on every parent change. You switch to `OnPush` and stabilize the update behavior.

Breakpoints in Browser DevTools

Use source maps (`sourceMap: true` in `angular.json`) to enable TypeScript debugging in Chrome or Firefox.

Set breakpoints by:

Opening the `.ts` file in the Sources tab.

Clicking the line number to place a breakpoint.

Reloading or triggering the code path.

Now you can:

Step through code line-by-line.

Hover over variables to inspect their values.

View the call stack to see what triggered the function.

Combine this with `console.trace()` when you want to log a stack without halting execution:

```
console.trace('Trace user click flow');
```

Leverage `debugger` Statements in Dev Mode

You can programmatically halt execution like this:

```
if (!environment.production) {

  debugger; // triggers the browser's devtools
pause

}
```

Use this in service callbacks, template events, or conditional branches that behave unexpectedly. It pauses the browser exactly where the bug occurs.

Debugging Change Detection Behavior

If a component is not updating the UI correctly:

Confirm `ChangeDetectionStrategy.OnPush` usage.

Check whether you're mutating an object instead of replacing it.

Manually call `markForCheck()` if you're updating state outside Angular's zone (e.g., from a 3rd party lib).

Check for Signals or `Observable` emissions—are they changing the tracked value?

Example of mutation that breaks detection:

```
this.user.name = 'Updated'; // won't trigger OnPush
```

Correct:

```
this.user = { ...this.user, name: 'Updated' }; //
triggers detection
```

Handling Uncaught Errors Gracefully

Angular provides a global error hook:

```
@Injectable()
export class GlobalErrorHandler implements
ErrorHandler {
  handleError(error: any): void {
    console.error('[GlobalErrorHandler] Uncaught
error:', error.message);
    // log to server, show toast, etc.
  }
}
```

Register in your app providers:

```
{ provide: ErrorHandler, useClass:
GlobalErrorHandler }
```

Now any error not caught by `try/catch`, observables, or guards is logged centrally.

Use this in combination with tools like **Sentry**, **LogRocket**, or **Firebase Crashlytics** to monitor production exceptions.

Monitor Network Calls

Use the **Network** tab in browser DevTools:

Verify that the request is sent (status, payload, URL).

Inspect the response—what was returned?

Check timing—was it slow, blocked, or cached?

If an API is failing:

Check the status code (401, 500, etc.).

Look for CORS errors or authentication issues.

Inspect the Authorization headers or query params.

Mocking APIs in development can help isolate frontend errors.

Handling Async Code with async/await and Observables

If using async/await, always use try/catch:

```
async login() {
  try {
    const res = await
this.authService.login(this.credentials);
    console.log('Login successful:', res);
  } catch (err) {
    console.error('Login failed:', err.message);
  }
}
```

With observables, always subscribe using subscribe({ next, error }) or use catchError() in the pipeline:

```
this.authService.login(email, password).pipe(

  catchError(err => {

    console.error('Login error:', err);

    return EMPTY;

  })

).subscribe();
```

This ensures nothing gets silently dropped.

Browser-Specific Debugging Tips

Use **device emulation** to test mobile rendering issues.

Use **localStorage/sessionStorage** tabs to inspect or reset client state.

Use **Performance** tab to profile rendering slowdowns and reflows.

Use **Console Filters** to show only logs, errors, or warnings.

You can also run Chrome with special flags to enable deep debugging or disable cache:

```
chrome --auto-open-devtools-for-tabs --disable-cache
```

Real-World Debugging Example

You're building a dashboard that shows orders in a table. The table shows no data, even though the API is working.

Step-by-step:

Console log the API response in the service—confirm it returns data.

Log the value passed to the table component.

Use Angular DevTools to verify that the input is correctly received.

Use a breakpoint to check if the table's `ngOnInit()` is running.

Confirm that the data is not empty at that point.

Realize that the table expects `orders: Order[]`, but the service returns `data: { orders: Order[] }`.

Fix:

```
this.orders = res.orders; // instead of this.orders = res;
```

This issue would've taken hours with guesswork. It takes minutes with structured debugging.

Debugging is not just a skill—it's a workflow. When you combine precise logging, runtime inspection, DevTools awareness, and Angular's structured utilities, you're equipped to isolate and fix issues systematically.

Chapter 10: Deploying, Securing, and Maintaining Angular Apps

Once your Angular application is feature-complete and passes tests, it's not ready to go live until it's correctly optimized, securely configured, and structured for long-term maintenance. A development build works in local environments, but production demands performance, reliability, security, and upgradability.

Angular gives you a complete set of tools to prepare your app for deployment—from production builds and service workers to route protection and structured versioning. In this chapter, you'll learn how to compile a performant, production-ready Angular app, how to secure it against common risks, and how to maintain it cleanly as Angular continues to evolve.

Production Build Process and Optimization Flags

The transition from development to production in Angular isn't just about running a different build command—it's about compiling your application for maximum performance, minimal payload size, and long-term maintainability. A development build includes extra tooling, verbose error messages, and debugging helpers. A production build strips those away and prepares your application to load fast, run efficiently, and behave securely in the user's browser.

Angular CLI handles much of this optimization automatically, but it's important to understand how the build process works under the hood, how to control it, and how to validate that your output is ready for real-world deployment.

Creating a Production Build with Angular CLI

The CLI provides a built-in `--configuration=production` flag to compile your Angular application in production mode:

```
ng build --configuration=production
```

You can also use the shorthand:

```
ng build --prod
```

This triggers a number of performance-focused operations, including:

Ahead-of-Time (AOT) compilation

Tree shaking

Code minification

CSS extraction

Environment variable replacement

Bundle hashing for caching

Dead code elimination via `buildOptimizer`

All these steps aim to make your app faster to load, lighter to parse, and less likely to expose sensitive development information.

Understanding What Happens During Production Builds

Let's break down what this build command actually does.

1. Ahead-of-Time (AOT) Compilation

Angular compiles your component templates and metadata into JavaScript functions *before* the browser ever sees them. This removes the need to ship Angular's compiler into your production bundle.

Your component:

```
@Component({
  selector: 'app-hero',
  template: `<h3>{{ hero.name }}</h3>`
})
export class HeroComponent {
  @Input() hero!: Hero;
}
```

Compiles down to optimized JS rendering instructions:

```
ɵɵtextInterpolate1('Hero: ', ctx.hero.name, '');
```

This results in faster boot times and smaller payloads.

2. Tree Shaking

Angular's build pipeline eliminates unused exports. If you have utility functions, services, or constants that aren't used in your templates or logic, they'll be removed from the final bundle.

Make sure you use **ESM syntax** and **pure functions** to enable tree shaking:

```
export function unusedFunction() { ... } // Will be
removed if never imported
```

3. Minification and Uglification

Your JS, CSS, and HTML are reduced to minimal syntax:

Long variable names become single letters.

Whitespace and comments are stripped.

Console statements are removed (unless manually preserved).

This shrinks your files significantly—sometimes by 70–80%.

4. Bundle Hashing and Output Splitting

Angular generates hashed filenames like:

```
main.8f3a72c5cc45d4e2.js

polyfills.1a2b3c4d.js

styles.0a1b2c.css
```

This allows for long-term caching by the browser. When you change code, the hash changes, triggering a fresh download.

Split output also means:

`main.js` contains app logic.

`vendor.js` contains third-party libs like RxJS.

`runtime.js` handles bootstrapping.

Customizing Production Settings in `angular.json`

You can fully control production optimizations under the `configurations.production` block of `angular.json`.

Here's a real example:

```json
"production": {
  "optimization": true,
  "outputHashing": "all",
  "sourceMap": false,
  "namedChunks": false,
  "extractLicenses": true,
  "vendorChunk": false,
  "buildOptimizer": true,
  "fileReplacements": [
    {
      "replace": "src/environments/environment.ts",
      "with":
"src/environments/environment.prod.ts"
    }
  ]
}
```

Let's go over what each flag does:

optimization: Enables AOT, minification, and dead code elimination.

outputHashing: Appends a hash to filenames ("all", "media", or "none").

sourceMap: Should be `false` in production to avoid exposing source code.

namedChunks: Keep this `false` to reduce output size.

extractLicenses: Extracts third-party license comments into a separate file.

vendorChunk: Set `false` to merge vendor libs into main for fewer requests.

buildOptimizer: Runs Angular-specific tree shaking and template optimization.

Replacing Environment Variables Automatically

Production builds should never include development secrets, mock APIs, or debug toggles. Angular CLI supports replacing your `environment.ts` file automatically during the build.

Default behavior:

In development: `src/environments/environment.ts`

In production: `src/environments/environment.prod.ts`

Define flags in the environment files:

```
// environment.ts
export const environment = {
  production: false,
  apiUrl: 'http://localhost:3000/api',
  debug: true
};
// environment.prod.ts
export const environment = {
  production: true,
  apiUrl: 'https://api.example.com',
  debug: false
};
```

This ensures the compiled app uses real services and disables debugging tools when shipped.

Verifying Bundle Size with `stats.json`

To see what your production build includes:

```
ng build --configuration=production --stats-json
```

Then visualize it with Webpack Bundle Analyzer:

`npx webpack-bundle-analyzer dist/your-app/stats.json`

This gives you:

A tree view of every module and its size

A breakdown of lazy-loaded chunks

The ability to identify and remove oversized imports

If you see a huge vendor chunk, you may be importing entire libraries instead of individual functions (e.g. using `import * as _ from 'lodash'` instead of `import cloneDeep from 'lodash/cloneDeep'`).

Serving the Production Build

Once built, the files are located in `dist/your-app-name`. You can serve them with any static server:

`npx http-server -p 4200 dist/your-app-name`

Or copy to:

Nginx (`/var/www/html`)

Apache (`/htdocs`)

Firebase Hosting (`firebase deploy`)

AWS S3, Azure Blob Storage, or Cloudflare Pages

Just make sure your server is configured to fallback to `index.html` for Angular's client-side routing:

```
location / {
  try_files $uri $uri/ /index.html;
}
```

Real-World Tip: Bundle Budget Alerts

Angular allows you to set size budgets in `angular.json` to warn or fail the build if a file grows too large:

```
"budgets": [
  {
    "type": "initial",
    "maximumWarning": "500kb",
    "maximumError": "1mb"
  },
  {
    "type": "anyComponentStyle",
    "maximumWarning": "6kb"
  }
]
```

This prevents unnoticed bloat and ensures your team optimizes regularly.

When you exceed a budget, you'll see:

WARNING in budgets, maximum exceeded for initial. Budget 500 kB was exceeded by 50 kB.

A production build in Angular is more than just a compact version of your app—it's the result of multiple deliberate optimizations. When used correctly, Angular's build system compiles, compresses, splits, and secures your application, ensuring that it loads fast, scales well, and performs smoothly under load.

Service Workers, PWA Support, and SSR

A performant Angular application isn't just defined by how quickly it renders after loading—it's defined by how reliably it behaves in real-world conditions. That includes handling slow or unreliable networks, being installable like a native app, and rendering content quickly even before JavaScript takes over.

To support these capabilities, Angular provides:

Service workers for caching assets and enabling offline functionality.

Progressive Web App (PWA) features for installability and enhanced mobile UX.

Server-Side Rendering (SSR) for improving first-load performance and enabling search engines to index content.

In this section, you'll learn how to integrate each of these technologies correctly in an Angular 19.2 application. The goal is to extend your application's reach beyond the browser's default behavior—providing offline access, SEO visibility, native-like user experience, and fast perceived performance.

Service Workers: Offline Support and Caching

A service worker is a script that the browser runs in the background, independent of your Angular application. It intercepts network requests and can serve cached versions of files or even API responses, allowing your app to function offline or on slow networks.

Angular provides first-class support for service workers through the `@angular/service-worker` package.

Step 1: Adding a Service Worker

You can enable service worker support by running:

```
ng add @angular/pwa
```

This automatically:

Installs `@angular/service-worker`

Updates `angular.json` to register the service worker in production builds

Adds a `manifest.webmanifest` for PWA features

Generates `ngsw-config.json` for service worker behavior

Step 2: Building with Service Worker Enabled

Run a production build:

```
ng build --configuration=production
```

This build includes the service worker in the `dist/` folder and injects registration logic into `main.ts`.

If you inspect the generated `main.ts`, you'll see:

```
if (environment.production) {
  enableProdMode();
}

platformBrowser().bootstrapModule(AppModule)
  .then(() => {
    if ('serviceWorker' in navigator &&
environment.production) {
      navigator.serviceWorker.register('ngsw-
worker.js');
    }
  });
```

Step 3: Understanding `ngsw-config.json`

This file controls what gets cached and how.

Example structure:

```
{
  "index": "/index.html",
  "assetGroups": [
    {
      "name": "app",
      "installMode": "prefetch",
      "resources": {
        "files": ["/favicon.ico", "/*.css",
"/*.js"]
      }
    },
    {
      "name": "assets",
      "installMode": "lazy",
      "resources": {
        "files": ["/assets/**"]
      }
    }
  ]
}
```

`installMode: prefetch` means the assets are cached immediately.

`installMode: lazy` means they are cached only when requested.

You can define fallback URLs and data groups as well.

To test service worker caching, serve with a static HTTP server:

```
npx http-server -p 8080 dist/your-app
```

Disconnect your network and reload the page—you'll see it still works using the service worker cache.

PWA Support: Making Your App Installable

A Progressive Web App is a web application that behaves like a native mobile or desktop application. To qualify as a PWA, your Angular app must:

Serve via HTTPS

Register a service worker

Include a valid `manifest.webmanifest`

The `@angular/pwa` package sets this up automatically.

Manifest Configuration

The `manifest.webmanifest` includes app metadata:

```
{
  "name": "AngularApp",
  "short_name": "App",
  "theme_color": "#1976d2",
  "background_color": "#fafafa",
  "display": "standalone",
  "scope": "/",
  "start_url": "/",
  "icons": [
    {
      "src": "assets/icons/icon-192x192.png",
      "sizes": "192x192",
      "type": "image/png"
    },
    {
      "src": "assets/icons/icon-512x512.png",
      "sizes": "512x512",
```

```
      "type": "image/png"
    }
  ]
}
```

Browsers that support PWA features will prompt users to "Install" the app when:

It's served over HTTPS

It has a valid service worker

It meets engagement thresholds (e.g., visited twice)

Once installed, the app can run standalone, without browser chrome.

Server-Side Rendering (SSR): Pre-Rendering Your Application

By default, Angular applications are client-side rendered—HTML is built dynamically in the browser. That means:

The initial HTML payload is mostly empty

Search engines and social crawlers may not index your app correctly

First meaningful paint is delayed while JavaScript loads

Server-Side Rendering solves this by rendering the app's HTML on the server and sending a complete page to the browser. After that, Angular takes over client-side.

Step 1: Add Angular Universal

Run the schematic:

ng add @nguniversal/express-engine

This will:

Create `app.server.module.ts`

Add server-specific entry files

Generate an Express server (`server.ts`)

Update `angular.json` with a `server` target

216

Step 2: Build for SSR

You need to build both the browser and server targets:

`npm run build:ssr`

This builds:

`/dist/browser` → browser bundle

`/dist/server` → server-side render bundle

To serve with SSR:

`npm run serve:ssr`

This starts an Express server on port 4000 by default. The server intercepts the request, renders the Angular component tree into HTML, and sends it to the browser.

Use cases:

Content-heavy marketing pages

Documentation, articles, product listings

SEO-sensitive routes (e.g., `/product/:id`, `/blog/:slug`)

Real-World Use Case: Combining All Three

Let's say you're building a public news platform with Angular:

You want articles indexed by Google (SSR).

You want users to be able to read cached content offline (Service Worker).

You want it to be installable and openable from home screens (PWA).

In that case:

Enable SSR for your article routes.

Cache static files and pre-fetched API data in the service worker.

Configure your manifest and icons for installability.

Use `AppShell` to provide a consistent skeleton for SSR and PWA startup.

The capabilities enabled by service workers, PWA features, and server-side rendering are not optional extras—they're essential for delivering resilient, responsive, and user-friendly Angular applications in today's web ecosystem.

To summarize:

Use service workers to cache assets and data for offline and low-bandwidth use.

Enable PWA support to let users install your app like a native experience.

Integrate SSR to improve SEO, performance, and perceived speed—especially for publicly accessible content.

Together, these technologies extend your Angular application beyond the browser tab—into the device, the home screen, the search index, and the hands of users who need reliability no matter the network condition.

Secure Authentication and Route Protection

When you build Angular applications that expose any form of personalized data or user-restricted access, security becomes a priority. It's not enough for your app to just show and hide buttons based on login state. Your routes must be protected, user tokens must be handled securely, and your API must not trust anything sent without validation.

In Angular 19.2, you have all the tools you need to build and enforce secure authentication workflows, whether you're integrating with OAuth providers, handling your own token-based login system, or protecting administrative panels from unauthorized access. This section will guide you through secure authentication handling, guarding routes effectively, protecting HTTP requests, and applying best practices for production-grade security.

Handling Authentication: Token-Based Login Flow

Most Angular applications authenticate against a backend that returns a token—typically a **JWT (JSON Web Token)**. That token is then stored on the client and attached to every subsequent request to prove the user's identity.

Here's a simplified login flow using Angular's `HttpClient` and RxJS:

Step 1: Building an Authentication Service

```
@Injectable({ providedIn: 'root' })
export class AuthService {
  private readonly tokenKey = 'auth_token';

  constructor(private http: HttpClient) {}

  login(email: string, password: string):
Observable<void> {
    return this.http.post<{ token: string
}>('https://api.example.com/login', {
      email,
      password
    }).pipe(
      tap(res =>
localStorage.setItem(this.tokenKey, res.token)),
      map(() => {})
    );
  }

  logout() {
    localStorage.removeItem(this.tokenKey);
  }

  isAuthenticated(): boolean {
    return !!localStorage.getItem(this.tokenKey);
  }

  getToken(): string | null {
    return localStorage.getItem(this.tokenKey);
  }
}
```

This service does the following:

Sends credentials to the backend.

Stores the JWT in `localStorage`.

Exposes a method to retrieve the token.

Provides a boolean indicating login state.

Important: **localStorage** is easy to use but vulnerable to XSS attacks. In high-security environments, consider **HttpOnly cookies** for token storage instead.

Protecting HTTP Requests with Interceptors

You don't want to manually attach tokens to every request. Use an Angular HttpInterceptor to handle this globally.

```
@Injectable()
export class AuthInterceptor implements
HttpInterceptor {
  constructor(private auth: AuthService) {}

  intercept(req: HttpRequest<any>, next:
HttpHandler) {
    const token = this.auth.getToken();

    if (token) {
      const authReq = req.clone({
        headers: req.headers.set('Authorization',
`Bearer ${token}`)
      });
      return next.handle(authReq);
    }

    return next.handle(req);
  }
}
```

Register the interceptor in your app module:

```
providers: [
  { provide: HTTP_INTERCEPTORS, useClass:
AuthInterceptor, multi: true }
]
```

Every outgoing request will now carry the token in the Authorization header. Your backend can validate this token and issue a 401 if it's invalid.

Handling Expired or Invalid Tokens

You can handle token errors within the same interceptor or in a separate one:

```
intercept(req: HttpRequest<any>, next:
HttpHandler): Observable<HttpEvent<any>> {
  return next.handle(req).pipe(
    catchError(error => {
      if (error.status === 401 || error.status ===
403) {
        this.auth.logout();
        this.router.navigate(['/login']);
      }
      return throwError(() => error);
    })
  );
}
```

This ensures that any unauthorized or expired token automatically logs the user out and redirects them to login.

Protecting Routes with Route Guards

Angular's `CanActivate` interface lets you prevent unauthorized users from accessing specific routes. This is crucial for protecting admin panels, user dashboards, and other restricted areas.

```
@Injectable({ providedIn: 'root' })
export class AuthGuard implements CanActivate {
  constructor(private auth: AuthService, private
router: Router) {}

  canActivate(): boolean {
    if (this.auth.isAuthenticated()) {
      return true;
    }

    this.router.navigate(['/login']);
    return false;
  }
}
```

Apply this to a route in your `app.routes.ts` or feature module:

```
{
  path: 'dashboard',
  component: DashboardComponent,
```

```
  canActivate: [AuthGuard]
}
```

This completely blocks unauthorized users from accessing the route—not just from seeing it, but from loading it entirely.

Protecting Lazy-Loaded Modules with `CanLoad`

You can also prevent lazy-loaded modules from being fetched at all using **CanLoad.**

```
@Injectable({ providedIn: 'root' })
export class AuthLoadGuard implements CanLoad {
  constructor(private auth: AuthService, private
router: Router) {}

  canLoad(): boolean {
    if (this.auth.isAuthenticated()) {
      return true;
    }

    this.router.navigate(['/login']);
    return false;
  }
}
```

Apply it like this:

```
{

  path: 'admin',

  loadChildren: () =>
import('./admin/admin.routes').then(m =>
m.ADMIN_ROUTES),

  canLoad: [AuthLoadGuard]

}
```

This adds another layer of protection by preventing the code for the `admin` module from even reaching the client.

Hiding UI Elements Based on Auth State

While guards block access to routes, you may also want to adjust the UI dynamically.

```
<nav *ngIf="auth.isAuthenticated()">

  <a routerLink="/dashboard">Dashboard</a>

  <a (click)="auth.logout()">Logout</a>

</nav>



<nav *ngIf="!auth.isAuthenticated()">

  <a routerLink="/login">Login</a>

</nav>
```

This ensures your layout reflects the authentication state without relying on route access alone.

For larger applications, use `BehaviorSubject` in `AuthService` to emit auth state reactively and subscribe in components.

Securing Login Forms and Error Handling

In your login component, validate inputs and guard against common errors like missing credentials or invalid submissions.

```
this.form = new FormGroup({
  email: new FormControl('', [Validators.required,
Validators.email]),
  password: new FormControl('',
Validators.required)
});
```

On submission:

```
this.auth.login(this.form.value.email,
this.form.value.password).subscribe({
```

```
  next: () => this.router.navigate(['/dashboard']),

  error: err => this.errorMessage = 'Login failed:
' + err.message

});
```

This ensures:

Form input is validated before sending.

Login errors don't crash the app.

Users receive feedback on what went wrong.

Real-World Strategy: JWT Expiration and Refresh Tokens

If your API issues short-lived JWTs, you'll need a refresh strategy.

Your backend should return:

```
{

  "access_token": "short-lived-jwt",

  "refresh_token": "long-lived-refresh"

}
```

Then in your `AuthService`, store both tokens securely. In your `AuthInterceptor`, detect token expiration and call the refresh endpoint automatically, then retry the original request.

This adds complexity but is required for long sessions without re-login.

Authentication is not just about showing the right screen—it's about making sure only valid users can access sensitive routes, use protected services, and persist session information securely across sessions.

Angular gives you the structure—you provide the discipline. Securing your routes and services properly is one of the clearest indicators that your application is ready for production and worthy of user trust.

Versioning, Upgrading to Future Releases, and Maintenance Tips

As your Angular application evolves, maintaining its stability while staying current with Angular's releases is not optional—it's a requirement. Angular follows a predictable release schedule, and with every major version, the framework introduces performance improvements, security patches, and new features that improve developer productivity and application performance. However, integrating these updates responsibly requires a disciplined versioning strategy and ongoing code maintenance practices.

Understanding Angular's Release Schedule and Lifecycle

Angular adheres to a **semantic versioning model** (semver) and a **scheduled release cycle**:

Two major releases per year (usually in March and September)

One active LTS (Long-Term Support) version at any time

Six months of active support, followed by **12 months of LTS** for each major release

Major versions introduce breaking changes—but these are always documented and accompanied by tooling and migration guidance. Minor and patch releases are safe to upgrade to at any time.

For example:

Angular 19 (March 2024): Feature release

Angular 20 (September 2024): New features + minor breaking changes

Angular 19 enters LTS when Angular 20 is released

You should aim to upgrade within one or two major versions to avoid falling behind and accumulating technical debt.

Semantic Versioning in `package.json`

Angular packages follow `MAJOR.MINOR.PATCH` versioning.

For example:

```
"dependencies": {

  "@angular/core": "19.2.3",

  "@angular/forms": "19.2.3",

  "@angular/router": "19.2.3"

}
```

You may also see versions prefixed with:

^ — allows updates to newer minor and patch versions (^19.2.3 upgrades to 19.x.x)

~ — allows only patch upgrades (~19.2.3 upgrades to 19.2.x)

No prefix — locks version exactly (19.2.3)

To ensure repeatable builds in CI environments, lock your core Angular dependencies exactly and rely on controlled updates rather than automatic ones.

Use npm ci in CI pipelines to install exact versions from package-lock.json.

Using ng update to Safely Upgrade Angular

Angular CLI provides an upgrade tool that evaluates your current setup and applies appropriate changes:

```
ng update
```

This command checks:

Which Angular packages are outdated

Compatibility between dependencies

Recommended versions to target

To upgrade core Angular packages:

ng update @angular/core @angular/cli

This will:

Update your `package.json`

Replace deprecated APIs where possible

Modify `angular.json` to reflect any new build options

Run migration scripts when needed

You can preview all available updates without applying them:

```
ng update --all --force --dry-run
```

Always commit your project before running `ng update` so you can revert easily if something breaks.

Using the Angular Update Guide

Angular provides an excellent interactive update guide:

https://update.angular.io

You select:

Your current version

Your target version

Whether you use Angular Material

Whether you're on a basic or complex project

It returns a checklist of:

CLI commands

Manual code changes

Deprecations to fix

Feature enhancements to adopt

Use this in conjunction with `ng update` for a complete upgrade strategy.

Handling Breaking Changes in Major Versions

Every major Angular release includes a changelog. You should review:

Deprecated APIs removed

Updated compiler options

Changes in default behavior

New syntax or patterns (e.g., signals, standalone APIs)

Examples of recent major updates:

Angular 15 introduced standalone components

Angular 16 introduced signals and zoneless reactivity

Angular 17 refined hydration for SSR

Angular 19 enhanced signal-based change detection

Breaking changes are **always opt-in** and rarely affect small projects. Still, they require attention during upgrades.

Real-World Upgrade Process Example

Suppose you're running Angular 17.0 and want to upgrade to 19.2.

Backup your code.

Update CLI and core packages:

```
ng update @angular/core@19 @angular/cli@19
```

Run unit tests and E2E tests:

```
ng test && ng e2e
```

Resolve deprecated APIs or schema warnings.

Upgrade third-party libraries:

```
ng update @angular/material @ngrx/store
```

Refactor any outdated patterns or module imports.

Commit all changes and update your deployment.

Long-Term Maintenance Best Practices

Upgrading Angular isn't the only maintenance work that matters. You should also:

1. Keep Dependencies Lean and Current

Run:

`npm outdated`

Remove unused libraries. Keep an eye on vulnerable packages:

`npm audit fix`

Only install libraries from reputable sources. Avoid packages with low stars, zero documentation, or no maintenance history.

2. Modularize Your Project

Split your codebase into:

Feature modules for isolated functionality

Shared modules for reused components and pipes

Core modules for singleton services

This makes upgrading easier and keeps your dependencies isolated. It also avoids circular imports and bloated bundles.

3. Document Decisions and Changes

Maintain:

A `CHANGELOG.md` for version-to-version changes

A `README.md` with environment setup, build, test, and deployment instructions

Comments explaining non-standard or "magic" logic

Clear documentation makes onboarding easier and prevents lost knowledge when team members change.

4. Automate Health Checks in CI

Your CI pipeline should include:

Linting with ESLint

Unit tests

Integration or E2E tests

Build budget enforcement

Example:

```
"budgets": [
  {
    "type": "initial",
    "maximumWarning": "500kb",
    "maximumError": "1mb"
  }
]
```

This prevents unnoticed bloat and protects against accidental regressions.

5. Clean Up and Refactor Regularly

Don't let old patterns accumulate. For example:

Migrate from `ngModules` to standalone APIs where possible

Replace deprecated lifecycle hooks or polyfills

Drop support for IE11 if still in code

Remove unused components, routes, and services

Small cleanup work now avoids painful rewrites later.

Angular is designed to be forward-compatible and well-supported—but that only helps if you stay proactive. Keeping your app updated protects it from security issues, keeps developer experience modern, and allows you to take advantage of new performance features.

Here's what to remember:

Lock and manage versions predictably using `package.json`

Use `ng update` with care and commit before applying changes

Upgrade regularly—don't skip multiple major versions

Modularize your code and keep it clean

Automate testing, auditing, and build-size enforcement

Your Angular application is a living system. If you treat versioning and maintenance as part of your development culture—not just something to do when it breaks—you'll keep it healthy, fast, and stable for years to come.

Appendices

Appendix A: Angular CLI Command Reference

Angular CLI (Command Line Interface) is the official tool for initializing, developing, testing, and building Angular applications. It provides a standardized workflow for projects of all sizes and enables consistent, repeatable tasks with simple commands. Whether you're generating new components or optimizing builds for production, the Angular CLI streamlines the development process.

This appendix provides a practical reference for common Angular CLI commands, complete with clear explanations and usage tips. These commands assume you're using Angular CLI version 15 and above, which includes support for standalone APIs and modern project structures.

1. Project Initialization and Setup

`ng new <project-name>`

Creates a new Angular project.

`ng new my-app`

Options:

`--standalone`: Uses standalone components and APIs.

`--routing`: Adds the Angular Router to the project.

`--style=scss`: Sets the stylesheet format (CSS, SCSS, etc.).

Example:

```
ng new dashboard --standalone --routing --
style=scss
```

This command generates the full directory structure, `angular.json`, and configuration files.

2. Serving the Application

ng serve

Compiles the app and starts a local development server.

ng serve

Default URL: `http://localhost:4200/`

Options:

`--port`: Changes the port number.

`--open`: Opens the app in the browser automatically.

`--configuration=production`: Serves the production build.

3. Building the Application

ng build

Compiles and bundles your application into the `dist/` directory.

ng build

Use the `--configuration=production` flag to enable optimizations like Ahead-of-Time (AOT) compilation, minification, and tree shaking.

ng build --configuration=production

This is the version you deploy to production servers.

4. Generating Code

The CLI can scaffold components, directives, services, pipes, guards, modules, and more.

ng generate component <name>

Creates a new component in the specified path.

ng generate component user/profile

Shortcut:

ng g c user/profile

Other generation commands:

```
ng g directive highlight

ng g service auth

ng g module admin

ng g guard auth

ng g pipe formatDate
```

Options:

`--standalone`: Generates a standalone component.

`--flat`: Prevents the creation of a subfolder.

`--skip-tests`: Omits the test file.

5. Running Tests

ng test

Runs unit tests using Karma.

ng test

Opens a browser window and watches for file changes. Test results are displayed live.

Options:

`--watch=false`: Runs tests once and exits (useful for CI).

ng e2e

Runs end-to-end tests. If using Cypress, this runs the Cypress test suite.

ng e2e

This command executes the configured E2E runner from **angular.json**.

6. Linting and Formatting

ng lint

Runs ESLint on your project files (if configured).

```
ng lint
```

Checks for code quality issues, formatting, and potential bugs.

Ensure you've migrated from TSLint to ESLint in Angular 12+ projects.

7. Updating Dependencies

```
ng update
```

Checks for outdated Angular dependencies and helps upgrade them safely.

```
ng update
```

To upgrade Angular core and CLI:

```
ng update @angular/core @angular/cli
```

Options:

`--force`: Bypasses version mismatches (use cautiously).

`--all`: Updates all packages (if compatible).

`--migrate-only`: Applies schematic changes without upgrading packages.

8. Configuration and Customization

```
ng config
```

Gets or sets values in `angular.json`.

```
ng config cli.defaultCollection

ng config
projects.myApp.architect.build.options.outputPath
dist/prod
```

You can also view full configuration:

```
ng config --global
```

9. Running Custom Scripts

```
ng run
```

Executes a named architect target (e.g., custom builders for deployment, prerendering, or SSR).

```
ng run my-app:build:production
```

Use this when invoking complex builders not covered by default commands.

10. Help and Documentation

ng help

Displays the full list of available commands.

```
ng help
```

For help on a specific command:

```
ng generate --help
```

This will list all options and examples for the `generate` command.

Angular CLI is designed to make development consistent, predictable, and efficient. It handles the underlying complexity of TypeScript, Webpack, RxJS, and the Angular compiler so you can focus on writing application logic.

Whether you're building a brand-new project, refactoring large features, or preparing for deployment, the CLI is your most reliable companion. Understanding its commands and knowing how to apply them saves time and reduces friction throughout the lifecycle of any Angular application.

Appendix B: RxJS Operators Cheat Sheet

RxJS (Reactive Extensions for JavaScript) is a library that provides tools for managing asynchronous data through **observables**—streams of data that you can observe and respond to over time. In Angular, RxJS is used extensively in HTTP communication, form handling, event binding, route activation, and reactive state management.

Operators in RxJS are functions that allow you to **transform**, **combine**, **filter**, or **control** the flow of data through an observable pipeline. These operators are typically used with the `pipe()` method and allow you to build clear, declarative logic for managing asynchronous operations.

236

This cheat sheet provides practical, beginner-friendly explanations of the most commonly used RxJS operators, grouped by their purpose.

1. Creation Operators

These operators are used to create new observables from static values, events, or other data structures.

of(...values)

Emits the provided values as a sequence.

```
of(1, 2, 3).subscribe(console.log); // 1, 2, 3

from(array | promise)
```

Converts an array, iterable, or promise into an observable.

```
from([10, 20, 30]).subscribe(console.log); // 10,
20, 30
interval(milliseconds)
```

Emits an incrementing number every specified time interval.

```
interval(1000).subscribe(console.log); // 0, 1, 2,
...
timer(delay, interval)
```

Starts emitting after a delay, then continues emitting at a given interval.

```
timer(2000, 1000).subscribe(console.log); // Starts
after 2s, then every 1s
```

2. Transformation Operators

These allow you to modify or reshape values as they flow through the observable.

map(fn)

Transforms each emitted value using the provided function.

```
of(1, 2, 3).pipe(map(x => x *
2)).subscribe(console.log); // 2, 4, 6
switchMap(fn)
```

Cancels the previous observable when a new value is emitted and switches to the new one. Useful for HTTP requests that should only use the latest input.

```
searchInput$.pipe(

  switchMap(query =>
http.get(`/api/search?q=${query}`))

).subscribe();

mergeMap(fn)
```

Runs all inner observables simultaneously and merges their results.

```
click$.pipe(

  mergeMap(() => http.get('/api/data'))

).subscribe();

concatMap(fn)
```

Queues each inner observable and waits for the current one to complete before subscribing to the next.

```
of(1, 2, 3).pipe(

  concatMap(id => http.get(`/api/item/${id}`))

).subscribe();
```

3. Filtering Operators

These let you control which values are allowed to continue through the pipeline.

filter(predicate)

Allows only values that pass a condition.

```
from([1, 2, 3, 4, 5]).pipe(

  filter(n => n % 2 === 0)
```

```
).subscribe(console.log); // 2, 4
debounceTime(milliseconds)
```

Waits for a pause in emissions before emitting the latest value. Useful for input fields.

```
input$.pipe(

   debounceTime(300)

).subscribe();

distinctUntilChanged()
```

Suppresses duplicate values that are the same as the previous.

```
of(1, 1, 2, 2,
3).pipe(distinctUntilChanged()).subscribe(); // 1,
2, 3

take(n)
```

Completes the observable after emitting n values.

```
interval(1000).pipe(take(3)).subscribe(); // emits
0, 1, 2 then completes
```

4. Combination Operators

These allow you to merge or combine multiple observables into one.

combineLatest([obs1, obs2, ...])

Emits the latest values from each observable when any of them emits.

```
combineLatest([obs1, obs2]).subscribe(([val1,
val2]) => {
   // val1 is latest from obs1, val2 is latest from
obs2
});
forkJoin([obs1, obs2, ...])
```

Waits for all observables to complete and then emits the last value from each.

```
forkJoin([http1$, http2$]).subscribe(([res1, res2])
=> {
    // Both HTTP requests are done
});
withLatestFrom(otherObs)
```

Emits the latest value from `otherObs` when the source observable emits.

```
click$.pipe(

  withLatestFrom(formValue$)

).subscribe(([click, formData]) => {

  // formData is the latest value at the moment of
the click

});
```

5. Error Handling Operators

Used to catch and handle errors in observable streams.

catchError(fn)

Catches an error and returns a new observable.

```
http.get('/api/data').pipe(

  catchError(err => of([])) // return fallback
value

).subscribe();

retry(n)
```

Retries the source observable up to `n` times when an error occurs.

```
http.get('/api/fetch').pipe(

  retry(3)

).subscribe();
```

6. Utility and Debugging Operators

These operators help observe or control the flow without modifying the data.

`tap(fn)`

Performs a side effect (like logging) without modifying the value.

```
source$.pipe(

  tap(value => console.log('Value:', value))

).subscribe();

finalize(fn)
```

Runs a callback when the observable completes or errors.

```
source$.pipe(

  finalize(() => console.log('Stream ended'))

).subscribe();
```

Using Operators in Angular

Here's how you typically use RxJS operators in Angular:

```
this.form.valueChanges.pipe(

  debounceTime(300),

  distinctUntilChanged(),

  switchMap(value => this.api.search(value)),

  catchError(() => of([]))

).subscribe(results => {

  this.searchResults = results;

});
```

This example:

Waits for the user to stop typing for 300ms

Ensures only changed values are sent

Cancels previous requests with `switchMap`

Handles errors gracefully

Updates the UI with search results

RxJS operators are the backbone of reactive programming in Angular. They give you precise control over asynchronous behavior, allowing you to express complex UI logic in a concise and readable way.

Appendix C: Signals API Reference (Stable in Angular 19.2)

The **Signals API** in Angular is a reactive programming feature that introduces a more explicit and efficient way to manage and respond to state changes. Unlike Angular's traditional change detection, which relies on zones and full component tree checks, Signals allow for **fine-grained reactivity** by tracking dependencies at the level of individual values.

As of Angular 19.2, the Signals API is **stable** and fully supported for production use. It offers an alternative to `@Input()`, `@Output()`, and manual subscriptions, and it can be used alongside existing observables or independently.

A **signal** is a reactive value that:

Holds state

Notifies dependents when the state changes

Triggers updates only where needed

Think of a signal like a special variable that Angular watches for changes, and automatically reacts to updates wherever that signal is used.

Creating and Using Signals

You create a signal using the `signal()` function:

```
import { signal } from '@angular/core';
```

```
const count = signal(0);
```

You can **read** the signal value by calling it like a function:

```
console.log(count()); // 0
```

You can **set** a new value:

```
count.set(5);
```

You can **update** it based on the previous value:

```
count.update(n => n + 1);
```

Computed Signals

A **computed signal** derives its value from one or more signals. It automatically recalculates when dependencies change.

```
import { computed } from '@angular/core';

const doubleCount = computed(() => count() * 2);

console.log(doubleCount()); // Updates
automatically as count changes
```

Computed signals are **read-only**—you can't call set() or update() on them.

Effects

An **effect** runs a function whenever any of the signals it uses change. It's typically used for side effects like logging or calling a service.

```
import { effect } from '@angular/core';

effect(() => {
  console.log('The count is:', count());
});
```

The effect re-runs only when count() changes. You don't need to manage subscriptions or teardown logic manually—Angular handles cleanup automatically.

Using Signals in Angular Components

You can declare and use signals inside Angular components just like any variable:

```
@Component({
  standalone: true,
  selector: 'counter',
  template: `
    <button
(click)="increment()">Increment</button>
    <p>Count: {{ count() }}</p>
  `
})
export class CounterComponent {
  count = signal(0);

  increment() {
    this.count.update(n => n + 1);
  }
}
```

You can bind to a signal in the template using parentheses (`count()`), just like calling a function. Angular will track this and re-render only when the signal changes.

Replacing `@Input()` with `input()`

Angular provides the `input()` function to reactively manage inputs as signals:

```
@Component({
  selector: 'user-badge',
  standalone: true,
  template: `<p>User: {{ userName() }}</p>`
})
export class UserBadgeComponent {
  userName = input<string>();
}
```

Then in the parent component:

```
<user-badge [userName]="'Jane Doe'"></user-badge>
```

This pattern makes inputs reactive and avoids manual `ngOnChanges` or lifecycle hooks.

244

Interoperability with Observables

You can convert from an observable to a signal using `toSignal()`:

```
import { toSignal } from '@angular/core/rxjs-
interop';

const data$ = this.http.get('/api/data');
const dataSignal = toSignal(data$);
```

`toSignal()` converts the observable into a signal that can be read and tracked like any other signal in templates or effects.

This is useful when you're working with existing observables and want to integrate them into the signal-based system.

Lifecycle and Cleanup

All signals and effects are **automatically disposed** when their scope is destroyed (e.g., when a component is destroyed). You don't need to unsubscribe manually, unlike RxJS.

This reduces memory leaks and simplifies logic, especially in components that depend on dynamic data or external state.

Best Practices with Signals

Prefer `signal()` for local component state instead of `BehaviorSubject`.

Use `computed()` for derived values instead of `map()` on observables when all dependencies are signal-based.

Use `effect()` for logic that affects external systems or has side effects (e.g., calling a service or updating the DOM).

Avoid mixing signal-based and observable-based patterns without a clear separation.

For form values and user input, signals often simplify state tracking and reduce boilerplate.

Limitations and Compatibility

Signals do not replace observables for asynchronous streams like HTTP or WebSockets.

You can't use signals directly in reactive forms; you'll still use `FormControl` or `formControlName` for form management.

Signals are not designed for multicast or stream replay—observables are still better for those scenarios.

The Signals API brings modern, reactive state management to Angular without the complexity of observable subscriptions or zone-based change detection. It enables local reactivity that is fast, explicit, and easy to maintain.

Use signals when:

You want fine-grained control over change detection.

You need reactive state in standalone components.

You want a lighter alternative to RxJS for local logic.

As of Angular 19.2, Signals are stable, production-ready, and supported natively in the framework. They're a powerful addition to the Angular developer's toolkit and are expected to play a central role in future Angular patterns and features.

Appendix D: Migration Guide from Angular 17/18 to 19.2

Angular 19.2 introduces several improvements to performance, developer ergonomics, and reactivity—most notably the stable release of the **Signals API**, enhancements to **standalone application architecture**, and updates to **dependency injection and hydration behavior**.

If you're working with an existing Angular 17 or 18 project, this guide will help you migrate your application safely and effectively. The process includes upgrading dependencies, reviewing breaking changes, and adopting new features in a controlled and testable way.

1. Preparation Before You Upgrade

Before you start the upgrade process, ensure your application is in a clean and stable state:

All unit and integration tests should pass.

Your `package.json` and `angular.json` should be free of custom overrides that conflict with Angular's defaults.

You should commit all changes and back up your project.

Also, ensure you're using **Node.js version 18.x or later**, as required by Angular 19.x.

2. Upgrade Angular CLI and Core Packages

Run the following command in your project root to upgrade the core Angular packages and CLI:

`ng update @angular/core@19 @angular/cli@19`

This command performs the following:

Updates your `package.json` to match Angular 19.x versions.

Applies schematics that automatically migrate deprecated usage where possible.

Adjusts your `angular.json` to align with new compiler targets and output options.

If you encounter version compatibility warnings (especially from third-party packages), resolve them before proceeding.

Use `--force` **only** if you're confident you can handle conflicts manually.

3. Update Angular Material and Other Dependencies (If Used)

If your project uses Angular Material or other Angular-specific libraries like NgRx, upgrade them with:

`ng update @angular/material`

`ng update @ngrx/store`

Consult each library's changelog to verify whether breaking changes or updated usage patterns exist in their latest release.

4. Adopt the Standalone APIs Where Appropriate

Angular 15+ introduced standalone components as an alternative to traditional `NgModules`. Angular 19 encourages continued use of this pattern.

If you're still using legacy modules for routing, bootstrapping, or feature encapsulation, you can begin refactoring them to use standalone components and imports.

For example:

```
@Component({

  standalone: true,

  selector: 'app-home',

  imports: [CommonModule],

  templateUrl: './home.component.html',

})
export class HomeComponent {}
```

Routing definitions now support standalone components directly:

```
const routes: Routes = [
  {
    path: '',
    component: HomeComponent // standalone
  }
];
```

Standalone APIs reduce boilerplate and improve clarity in feature module design.

5. Use Signals for Local State (If Appropriate)

Angular 19.2 marks the **Signals API** as stable. This API allows you to replace `BehaviorSubject`, component class properties, and `@Input()`/`@Output()` bindings with fine-grained reactive primitives.

For example, replace this:

```
count = 0;
```

```
increment() {
  this.count++;
}
```

With:

```
count = signal(0);

increment() {
  this.count.update(n => n + 1);
}
```

Use `input()` for reactive inputs:

```
import { input } from '@angular/core';

userId = input<number>();
```

Signals are fully supported in templates (`{{ count() }}`) and do not require zones to trigger updates. While you don't need to rewrite your entire application, consider using signals for new features or performance-sensitive areas.

6. Review Changes to Hydration and SSR (If Applicable)

Angular 18 introduced significant improvements to **server-side rendering (SSR)** and **hydration**, and Angular 19 further improves those capabilities.

If you're using Angular Universal:

Ensure your `@angular/platform-server` and `@angular/ssr` packages are up to date.

The hydration engine now works better with signals, standalone components, and `ng-container`-based layouts.

There is no manual migration needed unless you're using custom SSR logic or patching the DOM manually.

For reference: Angular's SSR and hydration features aim to render the initial page server-side, then hydrate the components client-side to keep them interactive without re-rendering from scratch.

7. Deprecations and Removals

Angular 19 removes support for deprecated APIs from earlier versions. If you see compiler warnings after the update, address them by:

Replacing removed lifecycle hooks or renamed APIs.

Updating any deprecated `Renderer2` usage.

Refactoring `ngOnDestroy` and `ngOnInit` logic into `effects` or signals where appropriate.

Use the Angular compiler messages as guidance—most include suggestions or direct links to updated documentation.

8. Validate and Test After the Upgrade

After updating, be sure to:

Run all unit tests:

ng test

Run E2E tests (if configured):

ng e2e

Manually verify complex workflows, lazy-loaded modules, and protected routes.

Fix any regressions before proceeding to use or deploy the upgraded app in production.

9. Optional: Enable Strict Defaults and Standalone by Default

For new projects or feature modules, consider enabling:

`strict: true` in `tsconfig.json` for better type safety.

`standalone: true` in schematic settings to prefer standalone components.

You can update your `angular.json` or `ng config` to reflect these changes:

```
ng config
schematics.@schematics/angular.component.standalone
true
```

Summary of Key Migration Steps

Backup your project and ensure it is test-stable.

Run `ng update @angular/core @angular/cli`.

Update Angular Material or other libraries.

Gradually refactor to standalone components where beneficial.

Use signals for local reactive state (optional but encouraged).

Verify SSR and hydration if applicable.

Remove deprecated code based on compiler warnings.

Test thoroughly before deployment.

Migrating from Angular 17 or 18 to 19.2 is straightforward for most projects. Angular's CLI tools and schematics handle most of the heavy lifting, and the framework's commitment to backward compatibility ensures smooth transitions with minimal disruption. That said, embracing new patterns like **standalone components**, **Signals**, and **fine-grained hydration** offers real benefits in performance, scalability, and maintainability.

Approach the upgrade iteratively, validate your code at each step, and use new features where they bring meaningful clarity or performance gains. This will help your application stay aligned with Angular's modern best practices.

Appendix E: Recommended Tools and Resources

The Angular ecosystem includes a wide range of tools and libraries designed to improve development speed, consistency, performance, testing, and deployment. Whether you're starting a new application or maintaining a production-scale system, selecting the right tools will help streamline your work and reduce long-term maintenance overhead.

This appendix lists and explains some of the most useful and widely adopted tools in the Angular ecosystem, grouped by their primary purpose. The goal is to provide a reliable set of recommendations that are appropriate for both new and experienced Angular developers.

1. Development and Debugging Tools

Angular DevTools

Angular DevTools is a browser extension available for Chrome and Firefox. It allows you to inspect Angular applications in real time, including:

Component trees

Signal and input values

Change detection activity

Performance profiling

It replaces the older Augury extension and works with Angular versions 12 and later.

 https://angular.dev/tools/devtools

Visual Studio Code (VS Code)

VS Code is the most commonly used editor for Angular development. It supports:

Angular TypeScript integration

IntelliSense for templates and components

Built-in terminal and Git support

Popular extensions such as ESLint, Prettier, Angular Language Service

Recommended Extensions:

Angular Language Service

ESLint

Prettier – Code formatter

Path Intellisense

 https://code.visualstudio.com

2. Linting, Formatting, and Quality Control

ESLint

ESLint is a static code analysis tool used to identify problematic patterns in JavaScript and TypeScript code. It is the current standard linter for Angular (replacing TSLint). Angular projects use `@angular-eslint` for CLI-compatible configurations.

You can run:

```
ng lint
```

To check your code for formatting and structural issues.

 https://eslint.org

Prettier

Prettier is an opinionated code formatter. It enforces consistent formatting of your TypeScript, JavaScript, HTML, and CSS.

It works well alongside ESLint, and you can run it using:

`npx prettier --write .`

 https://prettier.io

3. Testing and Automation

Jest

Jest is a fast, modern JavaScript testing framework. Though Angular defaults to Karma, many teams use Jest for faster test execution and simpler configuration.

Use `jest-preset-angular` for Angular support.

 https://jestjs.io

Cypress

Cypress is an end-to-end testing framework for frontend applications. It runs tests in the browser, with:

Real-time feedback

Automatic waiting

Screenshots and video recordings

It's highly recommended for testing UI behavior, routing, forms, and state transitions.

 https://www.cypress.io

Playwright

Playwright is another E2E testing tool like Cypress, but designed to support multi-browser automation. It's useful for teams that need testing across Chromium, Firefox, and WebKit.

 https://playwright.dev

4. State Management and Utilities

NgRx

NgRx is a reactive state management library inspired by Redux. It's suitable for large applications with shared, predictable state logic.

Includes:

Store (state container)

Effects (side effects)

Entity (normalized data handling)

SignalStore (optional modern API for Signals)

 https://ngrx.io

Akita

Akita is another state management library, designed to be simpler and more object-oriented than NgRx. It provides stores, queries, and devtools integration.

 https://datorama.github.io/akita

5. Build and Deployment Tools

Nx (Nrwl)

Nx is a powerful build system and monorepo toolkit. It provides smart project graph analysis, code generation, and caching to speed up builds and enforce structure in larger Angular codebases.

Nx supports:

Affected builds

Workspace generators

Dependency graph visualization

 https://nx.dev

Angular Universal

For server-side rendering (SSR), Angular Universal enables Angular applications to render on the server before being sent to the client. It improves load performance and supports SEO requirements.

 https://angular.io/guide/universal

Firebase Hosting

Firebase offers simple and secure static hosting for Angular apps, with built-in support for SSR, authentication, and serverless functions.

```
firebase deploy
```

 https://firebase.google.com

6. Documentation and Learning Resources

Official Angular Documentation

Always start here. The official documentation is regularly updated, includes guides, API references, and upgrade paths.

⊘ https://angular.io

RxJS Documentation

The official RxJS site offers examples, API reference, and marble diagrams for better understanding stream behavior.

⊘ https://rxjs.dev

Angular Update Guide

This tool helps you plan framework upgrades and provides tailored instructions for your current version.

⊘ https://update.angular.io

Angular YouTube Channel

Angular's official YouTube channel offers weekly updates, live coding sessions, and in-depth explorations of new features.

⊘ https://www.youtube.com/angular

Angular provides a strong foundation, but it's the surrounding ecosystem that shapes your development workflow. These tools—when chosen appropriately for your team and project size—can help you improve development speed, prevent errors, automate common tasks, and scale confidently.

Keep your tools updated, adopt ones that solve real problems in your workflow, and follow official sources to stay aligned with Angular's evolution.